ALSO BY NORA EPHRON

FICTION
Heartburn

ESSAYS
Nora Ephron Collected
Scribble Scribble
Crazy Salad
Wallflower at the Orgy

DRAMA
Imaginary Friends

SCREENPLAYS
Bewitched (with Delia Ephron)
Hanging Up (with Delia Ephron)
You've Got Mail (with Delia Ephron)
Michael (with Jim Quinlan, Pete Dexter, and Delia Ephron)
Mixed Nuts (with Delia Ephron)
Sleepless in Seattle (with David S. Ward and Jeff Arch)
This Is My Life (with Delia Ephron)
My Blue Heaven
When Harry Met Sally
Cookie (with Alice Arlen)
Heartburn
Silkwood (with Alice Arlen)

I Feel Bad About My Neck

I Feel Bad About My Neck

AND OTHER THOUGHTS ON BEING A WOMAN

Nora Ephron

 Alfred A. Knopf   *New York*   2006

THIS IS A BORZOI BOOK
PUBLISHED BY ALFRED A. KNOPF

Copyright © 2006 by Nora Ephron

www.aaknopf.com

Some of the essays in this collection
have previously appeared in the following:
"I Hate My Purse" in *Harper's Bazaar;*
"Moving On" and "Serial Monogamy" in *The New Yorker;*
"The Lost Strudel," "Me and Bill: The End of Love," and
"Me and JFK: Now It Can Be Told" in *The New York Times;*
"Where I Live" in *O, At Home;*
"On Maintenance" and "On Rapture" in *O, The Magazine;* and
"Considering the Alternative" and "I Feel Bad About My Neck" in *Vogue.*

Library of Congress Cataloging-in-Publication Data
Ephron, Nora.
I feel bad about my neck :
and other thoughts on being a woman / Nora Ephron.—
1st. ed.
p. cm.
ISBN 0-307-26455-6 (alk. paper)
1. Ephron, Nora. I. Title.
PS3555.P5I23 2006   2005057780
814'.54—dc22

Manufactured in the United States of America
Published August 3, 2006
Reprinted Two Times
Fourth Printing, August 2006

For Nick, Jacob, and Max

Contents

I Feel Bad About My Neck   3

I Hate My Purse   9

Serial Monogamy: A Memoir   17

On Maintenance   31

Blind as a Bat   50

Parenting in Three Stages   54

Moving On   65

Me and JFK: Now It Can Be Told   85

Contents

Me and Bill: The End of Love   90

Where I Live   94

The Story of My Life
in 3,500 Words or Less   97

The Lost Strudel or *Le Strudel Perdu*   112

On Rapture   117

What I Wish I'd Known   123

Considering the Alternative   127

Acknowledgments   139

I Feel Bad About My Neck

I Feel Bad About My Neck

I feel bad about my neck. Truly I do. If you saw my neck, you might feel bad about it too, but you'd probably be too polite to let on. If I said something to you on the subject—something like "I absolutely cannot stand my neck"—you'd undoubtedly respond by saying something nice, like "I don't know what you're talking about." You'd be lying, of course, but I forgive you. I tell lies like that all the time—mostly to friends who tell me they're upset because they have little pouches under their eyes, or jowls, or wrinkles, or flab around the middle, and do I think they should have an eye job, or a face-lift, or Botox, or liposuction. My experience is that "I don't know what you're talking about" is code for "I see what you mean, but if you think you're going to trap me into engaging on this subject, you're crazy." It's dangerous to engage on such subjects, and we all know it. Because if I said, "Yes, I see exactly what you mean," my friend might go out and have her eyes done, for instance, and it might not work, and she might end up being one of those people you read about in tabloids who ends up in court suing their plastic surgeons because they can never close their eyes again. Furthermore, and this is the point: It would be All My Fault. I am particularly sensitive to the All My Fault aspect of things, since I have never forgiven one of my friends for telling me not to buy a perfectly good apartment on East Seventy-fifth Street in 1976.

Sometimes I go out to lunch with my girlfriends— I got that far into the sentence and caught myself. I suppose I mean my women friends. We are no longer girls and have not been girls for forty years. Anyway, sometimes we go out to lunch and I look around the table and realize we're all wearing turtleneck sweaters. Sometimes, instead, we're all wearing scarves, like Katharine Hepburn in *On Golden Pond*. Sometimes we're all wearing mandarin collars and look like a white ladies' version of the Joy Luck Club. It's sort of funny and it's sort of sad, because we're not neurotic about age—none of us lies about how old she is, for instance, and none of us dresses in a way that's inappropriate for our years. We all look good for our age. Except for our necks.

Oh, the necks. There are chicken necks. There are turkey gobbler necks. There are elephant necks. There are necks with wattles and necks with creases that are on the verge of becoming wattles. There are scrawny necks and fat necks, loose necks, crepey necks, banded necks, wrinkled necks, stringy necks, saggy necks, flabby necks, mottled necks. There are necks that are an amazing combination of all of the above. According to my dermatologist, the neck starts to go at forty-three, and that's that. You can put makeup on your face and concealer under your eyes and dye on your hair, you can shoot collagen and Botox and Restylane into your wrinkles and creases, but short of surgery, there's not a damn thing you can do about a neck. The neck is a dead giveaway. Our faces are lies and our necks are the truth. You have to cut open a redwood tree to see how old it is, but you wouldn't have to if it had a neck.

My own experience with my neck began shortly before I turned forty-three. I had an operation that left me with a terrible scar just above the collarbone. It was shocking, because I learned the hard way that just because a doctor was a famous surgeon didn't mean he had any gift for sewing people up. If you learn nothing else from reading this essay, dear reader, learn this: Never have an operation on any part of your body without asking a plastic surgeon to come stand by in the operating room and keep an eye out. Because even if you are being operated on for something serious or potentially serious, even if you honestly believe that your health is more important than vanity, even if you wake up in the hospital room thrilled beyond imagining that it wasn't cancer, even if you feel elated, grateful to be alive, full of blinding insight about what's important and what's not, even if you vow to be eternally joyful about being on the planet Earth and promise never to complain about anything ever again, I promise you that one day soon, sooner than you can imagine, you will look in the mirror and think, I hate this scar.

Assuming, of course, that you look in the mirror. That's another thing about being a certain age that I've noticed: I try as much as possible not to look in the mirror. If I pass a mirror, I avert my eyes. If I must look into it, I begin by squinting, so that if anything really bad is looking back at me, I am already halfway to closing my eyes to ward off the sight. And if the light is good (which I hope it's not), I often do what so many women my age do when stuck in front of a mirror: I gently pull the skin of my neck back and stare wistfully at a younger version of myself. (Here's something else I've noticed, by the way: If you want to get really, really depressed about your neck, sit in the backseat of a car, right behind the driver, and look at yourself in the rearview mirror. What is it about rearview mirrors? I have no idea why, but there are no worse mirrors where necks are concerned. It's one of the genuinely compelling mysteries of modern life, right up there with why the cold water in the bathroom is colder than the cold water in the kitchen.)

But my neck. This is about my neck. And I know

what you're thinking: Why not go to a plastic surgeon? I'll tell you why not. If you go to a plastic surgeon and say, I'd like you just to fix my neck, he will tell you flat out that he can't do it without giving you a face-lift too. And he's not lying. He's not trying to con you into spending more money. The fact is, it's all one big ball of wax. If you tighten up the neck, you've also got to tighten up the face. But I don't want a face-lift. If I were a muffin and had a nice round puffy face, I would bite the bullet—muffins are perfect candidates for this sort of thing. But I am, alas, a bird, and if I had a face-lift, my neck would be improved, no question, but my face would end up pulled and tight. I would rather squint at this sorry face and neck of mine in the mirror than confront a stranger who looks suspiciously like a drum pad.

Every so often I read a book about age, and whoever's writing it says it's great to be old. It's great to be wise and sage and mellow; it's great to be at the point where you understand just what matters in life. I can't stand people who say things like this. What can they be thinking? Don't they have necks? Aren't they tired of compensatory dressing? Don't they mind that 90 percent of the clothes they might otherwise buy have to be eliminated simply because of the necklines? Don't they feel sad about having to buy chokers? One of my biggest regrets—bigger even than not buying the apartment on East Seventy-fifth Street, bigger even than my worst romantic catastrophe—is that I didn't spend my youth staring lovingly at my neck. It never crossed my mind to be grateful for it. It never crossed my mind that I would be nostalgic about a part of my body that I took completely for granted.

Of course it's true that now that I'm older, I'm wise and sage and mellow. And it's also true that I honestly do understand just what matters in life. But guess what? It's my neck.

I Hate My Purse

I hate my purse. I absolutely hate it. If you're one of those women who think there's something great about purses, don't even bother reading this because there will be nothing here for you. This is for women who hate their purses, who are bad at purses, who understand that their purses are reflections of negligent house-keeping, hopeless disorganization, a chronic inability to throw anything away, and an ongoing failure to handle the obligations of a demanding and difficult accessory (the obligation, for example, that it should in some way match what you're wearing). This is for women whose purses are a morass of loose Tic Tacs, solitary Advils, lipsticks without tops, ChapSticks of unknown vintage, little bits of tobacco even though there has been no smoking going on for at least ten years, tampons that have come loose from their wrappings, English coins from a trip to London last October, boarding passes from long-forgotten airplane trips, hotel keys from God-knows-what hotel, leaky ballpoint pens, Kleenexes that either have or have not been used but there's no way to be sure one way or another, scratched eyeglasses, an old tea bag, several crumpled personal checks that have come loose from the checkbook and are covered with smudge marks, and an unprotected toothbrush that looks as if it has been used to polish silver.

This is for women who in mid-July realize they still haven't bought a summer purse or who in midwinter are still carrying around a straw bag.

This is for women who find it appalling that a purse might cost five or six hundred dollars—never mind that top-of-the-line thing called a Birkin bag that costs ten thousand dollars, not that it's relevant because you can't even get on the waiting list for one. On the waiting list! For a purse! For a ten-thousand-dollar purse that will end up full of old Tic Tacs!

This is for those of you who understand, in short, that your purse is, in some absolutely horrible way, you. Or, as Louis XIV might have put it but didn't because he was much too smart to have a purse, *Le sac, c'est moi.*

I realized many years ago that I was no good at

purses, and for quite a while I managed to do without one. I was a freelance writer, and I spent most of my time at home. I didn't need a purse to walk into my own kitchen. When I went out, usually at night, I frequently managed with only a lipstick, a twenty-dollar bill, and a credit card tucked into my pocket. That's about all you can squeeze into an evening bag anyway, and it saved me a huge amount of money because I didn't have to buy an evening bag. Evening bags, for reasons that are obscure unless you're a Marxist, cost even more than regular bags.

But unfortunately, there were times when I needed to leave the house with more than the basics. I solved this problem by purchasing an overcoat with large pockets. This, I realize, turned my coat into a purse, but it was still better than carrying a purse. Anything is better than carrying a purse.

Because here's what happens with a purse. You start small. You start pledging yourself to neatness. You start vowing that This Time It Will Be Different. You start with the things you absolutely need—your wallet and a few cosmetics that you have actually put into a brand-new shiny cosmetics bag, the kind used by your friends who are competent enough to manage more than one purse at a time. But within seconds, your purse has accumulated the debris of a lifetime. The cosmetics have somehow fallen out of the shiny cosmetics bag (okay, you forgot to zip it up), the coins have fallen from the wallet (okay, you forgot to fasten the coin compartment), the credit cards are somewhere in the abyss (okay, you forgot to put your Visa card back into your wallet after you bought the sunblock that is now oozing into the lining because you forgot to put the top back onto it after you applied it to your hands while driving seventy miles an hour down the highway). What's more, a huge amount of space in your purse is being taken up by a technological marvel that holds your address book and calendar—or would, but the batteries in it have died. And there's half a bottle of water, along with several snacks you saved from an airplane trip just in case you ever found yourself starving and unaccountably craving a piece of cheese that tastes like plastic. Perhaps you can fit your sneakers into your purse. Yes, by God, you can! Before you know it, your purse weighs twenty pounds and you are in grave danger of getting bursitis and needing an operation just from carrying it around. Everything you own is in your purse. You could flee the Cossacks with your purse. But when you open it up, you can't find a thing in it—your purse is just a big dark hole full of stuff that you spend hours fishing around for. A flashlight would help, but if you were to put one into your purse, you'd never find it.

What's the solution? I'm no longer a freelance writer who sits home all day; I need stuff. I need stuff for work. I need cosmetics to tide me over. I need a book to keep me company. I need, sad to say, a purse. For a while, I searched for an answer. Like those Hollywood women who are willing to fling themselves into the Kabbalah, or Scientology, or yoga, I read just about any article about purses that promised me some sort of salvation from this misery. At one point I thought, Perhaps the solution is not one purse but two. So I tried having two purses, one for personal things and one for work things. (Yes, I know: The second purse is usually called a briefcase.) This system works for most people but not for me, and for a fairly obvious reason, which I've already disclosed: I'm not an organized human being. Another solution I tried involved spending quite a lot of money on a purse, on the theory that having an expensive purse would inspire me to change my personality, but that didn't work either. I also tried one of those Prada-style semi-backpack purses, but I bought it just when it was going out of fashion, and in any case I put so much into it that I looked like a sherpa.

And then, one day, I found myself in Paris with a friend who announced that her goal for the week was to buy a Kelly bag. Perhaps you know what a Kelly bag is. I didn't. I had never heard of one. What is a Kelly bag? I asked. My friend looked at me as if I had spent the century asleep in a cave. And she explained: A Kelly bag is an Hermès bag first made in the 1950s that Grace Kelly had made famous; hence the name. It is a classic. It is the purse equivalent of the world's most perfect string of pearls. It's still being manufactured, but my friend didn't want a new one, she wanted a vintage Kelly bag. She'd heard that there was a dealer in the flea market who had several for sale. The flea market is open on weekends only, so we spent several days eating, drinking, sightseeing, all of it (as far as my friend was concerned) mere prelude to the main event. How much is this purse going to cost? I asked. I practically expired when she told me: about three thousand dollars. Three thousand dollars for an old purse, plus (if you're counting, which I was) plane fare?

Well, finally we went to the flea market and there was the Kelly bag. I didn't know what to say. It looked like the sort of bag my mother used to carry. It barely held anything, and it hung stiffly on my friend's arm. I may not be good at purses, but I know that any purse that hangs stiffly on your arm (instead of on your shoulder) adds ten years to your age, and furthermore immobilizes half your body. In a modern world, your arms have to be free. I don't want to get too serious here, but a purse (like a pair of high heels) actually impinges on your mobility. That's one of many reasons why you don't see the guys-with-purses trend catching on. If one of your hands is stuck carrying your purse, it means it's not free for all sorts of exciting things you could be using it for, like shoving your way through crowds, throwing your arms around loved ones, climbing the greasy pole to success, and waving madly for taxis.

Anyway, my friend bought her Kelly bag. She paid twenty-six hundred dollars for it. The color wasn't exactly what she wanted, but it was in wonderful shape. Of course it would have to be waterproofed immediately because it would lose half its value if it got caught in the rain. Waterproofed? Caught in the rain? It had never crossed my mind to worry about a purse being caught in the rain, much less being waterproofed. For a moment I thought once again about how my mother had failed to teach me anything about purses, and I almost felt sorry for myself. But it was time for lunch.

The two of us went to a bistro, and the Kelly bag was placed in the center of the table, where it sat like a small shrine to a shopping victory. And then, outside, it began to rain. My friend's eyes began to well with tears. Her lips closed tightly. In fact, to be completely truthful, her lips actually *pursed*. It was pouring rain and she hadn't had the Kelly bag waterproofed. She would have to sit there all afternoon and wait for the rain to end rather than expose the bag to a droplet of moisture. It crossed my mind that she and her Kelly bag might have to sit there forever. Years would pass and the rain would continue to fall. She would get old (although her Kelly bag would not) and eventually she and the bag would, like some modern version of Lot's wife, metamorphose into a monument to what happens to people who care too much about purses. Country songs would be written about her, and parables. At that point I stopped worrying about purses and gave up.

I came back to New York and bought myself a purse. Well, it's not a purse exactly; it's a bag. It's definitely the best bag I have ever owned. On it is the image of a New York City MetroCard—it's yellow (taxicab yellow, to be exact) and blue (the most horrible blue of all, royal blue)—so it matches nothing at all and therefore, on a deep level, matches everything. It's made of plastic and is therefore completely waterproof. It's equally unattractive in all seasons of the year. It cost next to nothing (twenty-six dollars), and I will never have to replace it because it seems to be completely indestructible. What's more, never having been in style, it can never go out of style.

It doesn't work for everything, I admit; on rare occasions, I'm forced to use a purse, one that I hate. But mostly I go everywhere with my MetroCard bag. And wherever I go, people say to me, I love that bag. Where did you get that bag? And I tell them I bought it at the Transit Museum in Grand Central station, and that all proceeds from it go toward making the New York City subway system even better than it is already. For all I know, they've all gone off and bought one. Or else they haven't. It doesn't matter. I'm very happy.

Serial Monogamy:
A Memoir

My mother gave me my first cookbook. It was 1962, and I began my New York life with her gift of *The Gourmet Cookbook* (volume 1) and several sets of sheets and pillowcases (white, with scallops). *The Gourmet Cookbook* was enormous, a tome, with a gloomy reddish brown binding. It was assembled by the editors of *Gourmet* magazine and punctuated by the splendid, reverent, slightly lugubrious pictures of food the magazine was famous for. Simply owning it had changed my mother's life. Until the book appeared, in the fifties, she had been content to keep as far from the kitchen as possible. We had a wonderful Southern cook named Evelyn Hall, who cooked American classics like roast beef and fried chicken and a world-class apple pie. But thanks to *The Gourmet Cookbook,* Evelyn began to cook chicken Marengo and crème caramel; before long, my mother herself was in the kitchen, whipping up Chinese egg rolls from scratch. A recipe for them appears on page 36 of the book, but it doesn't begin to convey how stressful and time-consuming an endeavor it is to make egg rolls, nor does it begin to suggest how much tension a person can create in a household by serving egg rolls that take hours to make and are not nearly as good as Chinese takeout.

Owning *The Gourmet Cookbook* made me feel tremendously sophisticated. For years I gave it to friends as a wedding present. It was an emblem of adulthood, a way of being smart and chic and college-educated where food was concerned, but I never really used it in the way you're supposed to use a cookbook—by propping it open on the kitchen counter, cooking from it, staining its pages with spattered butter and chocolate splotches, conducting a unilateral dialogue with the book itself—in short, by having a relationship with it.

The cookbook I used most my first year in New York was a small volume called *The Flavour of France.* It was given to me by a powerful older woman I'll call Jane, whom I met my first summer in the city. She was twenty-five, and she took me in hand and introduced me not just to the cookbook but also to Brie and *vitello ton-*

nato and the famous omelet place in the East Sixties. In fact, the first time I went to the omelet place, which was called Madame Romaine de Lyon, I was a mail girl at *Newsweek,* making fifty-five dollars a week, and I almost fainted when I saw that an omelet cost $3.45. Jane also introduced me to the concept of One Away. You were One Away from someone if you had both slept with the same man. Jane had slept with a number of up-and-coming journalists, editors, and novelists, the most famous of whom, at the end of their one night together, gave her a copy of one of his books, a box of which was conveniently located right next to his front door. According to Jane, his exact words, as she made her way to the exit, were "Take one on your way out."

The night President Kennedy was shot, Jane was having a dinner party, which went forward in spite of the tragedy, as these things tend to do. Jane served as an appetizer *céleri rémoulade,* a dish that I had never before encountered and that remains a mystery to me. A few months later, I had a thing with someone Jane had had a thing with. Jane and I were now One Away from each other, and interestingly, that was the end of our friendship, though not the end of my connection to *The Flavour of France.*

The Flavour of France was the size of a date book, only six by eight inches. It contained small blocks of recipe text by Narcissa Chamberlain and her daughter Narcisse, and large black-and-white travel photographs of France taken by Narcissa's husband (and Narcisse's father), Samuel Chamberlain. I didn't focus much on the mysterious Chamberlain family as I cooked my way through their cookbook, and when I did, I usually hit a wall. For openers, I couldn't imagine why anyone named Narcissa would name her daughter Narcisse. Also, I couldn't figure out how they collaborated. Did the three of them drive around France together, fighting over whose turn it was to sit in the backseat? Did Narcisse like working with her parents? And if so, was she crazy? But the Chamberlains' recipes were simple and foolproof. I learned to make a perfect chocolate mousse that took about five minutes, and a wonderful dessert of caramelized baked pears with cream. I made those pears for years, although chocolate mousse eventually faded from my repertory when the crème brûlée years began.

Just before I'd moved to New York, two historic events had occurred: The birth control pill had been invented, and the first Julia Child cookbook was published. As a result, everyone was having sex, and when the sex was over, you cooked something. One of my girlfriends moved in with a man she was in love with. Her mother was distraught and warned that he would never marry her because she had already slept with him. "Whatever you do," my friend's mother said, "don't cook for him." But it was too late. She cooked for him. He married her anyway. This was right around the time endive was discovered, which was followed by arugula, which was followed by radicchio, which was followed by frisée, which was followed by the three *M*'s—mesclun, mâche, and microgreens—and that, in a nutshell, is the history of the last forty years from the point of view of lettuce. But I'm getting ahead of the story.

By the mid-sixties, Julia Child's *Mastering the Art of French Cooking,* Craig Claiborne's *New York Times Cookbook,* and *Michael Field's Cooking School* had become the holy trinity of cookbooks. At this point I was working as a newspaper reporter at the *New York Post* and living in the Village. If I was home alone at night, I cooked myself an entire meal from one of these cookbooks. Then I sat down in front of the television set and ate it. I felt very brave and plucky as I ate my perfect dinner. Okay, I didn't have a date, but at least I wasn't one of those lonely women who sat home with a pathetic container of yogurt. Eating an entire meal for four that I had cooked for myself was probably equally pathetic, but that never crossed my mind.

I cooked every single recipe in Michael Field's book and at least half the recipes in the first Julia, and as I cooked, I had imaginary conversations with them both. Julia was nicer and more forgiving—she was by then on television and famous for dropping food, picking it up, and throwing it right back into the pan. Michael Field was sterner and more meticulous; in fact, he was almost fascistic. He was full of prejudice about things like the garlic press (he believed that using one made the garlic bitter), and I threw mine away for fear he would suddenly materialize in my kitchen and disapprove. His recipes were precise, and I followed them to the letter; I was young, and I believed that if you changed even a hair on a recipe's head, it wouldn't turn out right. When I had people to dinner, I loved to serve Michael's complicated recipe for chicken curry, accompanied by condiments and pappadums—although I sometimes served instead a marginally simpler Craig Claiborne recipe for lamb curry that had appeared in Craig's Sunday column in *The New York Times Magazine*. There were bananas in it, and heavy cream. I made it recently and it was horrible.

Craig Claiborne worked at *The New York Times* not just as the chief food writer but also as the restaurant critic; he was enormously powerful and influential, and I developed something of an obsession with him. Craig—everyone called him Craig even if they'd never met the man—was famous for championing ethnic cuisine, and as his devoted acolyte, I learned to cook things like moussaka and tabbouleh. Everyone lived for his Sunday recipes; it was the first page I turned to in the Sunday *Times*. Everyone knew he had a Techbuilt house on the bay in East Hampton, that he'd added a new kitchen to it, that he usually cooked with the French chef Pierre Franey, and that he despised iceberg lettuce. You can't really discuss the history of lettuce in the last forty years without mentioning Craig; he played a seminal role. I have always had a weakness for iceberg lettuce with Roquefort dressing, and that's one of the things I used to have imaginary arguments with Craig about.

For a long time, I hoped that Craig and I would meet and become friends. I gave a lot of thought to this eventuality, most of it concerning what I would cook if he came to my house for dinner. I was confused about whether to serve him something from one of his cookbooks or something from someone else's cookbook. Perhaps there was a protocol for such things; if so, I didn't know what it was. It occurred to me that I ought to serve him something that was "my" recipe, but I didn't have any recipes that were truly mine—with the possible exception of my mother's barbecue sauce, which mostly consisted of Heinz ketchup. But I desperately wanted him to come over. I'd read somewhere that people were afraid to invite him to dinner. I wasn't; I just didn't know the man. I must confess that my fantasy included the hope that after he came to dinner, he would write an article about me and of course include my recipes; but as I said, I didn't have any.

Meanwhile, we all began to cook in a wildly neurotic and competitive way. We were looking for applause, we were constantly performing, we were desperate to be all things to all people. Was this the grand climax of the post–World War II domestic counterrevolution or the beginning of a pathological strain of feminist overreaching? No one knew. We were too busy slicing and dicing.

I got married and entered into a series of absolutely insane culinary episodes. I made the Brazilian national dish. I wrapped things in phyllo. I stuffed grape leaves. There were soufflés. I took a course in how to use a Cuisinart food processor. I even cooked an entire Chinese banquet that included Lee Lum's lemon chicken. Lee Lum was the chef at Pearl's, the famous Chinese restaurant where no one could get a table. If you did get a table, you remembered the meal forever because there was so much MSG in the food that you were awake for years afterward. Lee Lum's recipe for lemon chicken involved dipping strips of chicken breast in water-chestnut flour, frying it, plunging it into a sauce that included crushed pineapple, and dousing the entire concoction with a one-ounce bottle of lemon extract. Once again, the recipe was from the Sunday *Times* column written by Craig Claiborne. Craig of course had no difficulty getting a table at Pearl's, and I looked forward to going there with him someday, after we had actually met and become close personal friends. I'd gone to Pearl's once and was stunned to discover that it was not only impossible to get a table if you weren't famous but that being famous was not enough—there were degrees of famous. There was famous enough to get a table, and then there was famous enough to get Pearl to come to the table to tell you the nightly specials, and then there was true fame, top-of-the-line fame, which was famous enough to get Pearl to allow you to order the sweet-and-pungent crispy fish. This was what it came down to in New York: You had to have pull to order a fish.

I became a freelance magazine writer. One of my first pieces, for *New York* magazine, was about Craig Claiborne and Michael Field, who turned out to be at war with each other. As a result, I met Craig Claiborne, and after the article appeared, he invited me to his house. What he served for dinner was not memorable, and in any case, I don't remember it. Then Claiborne came to our house for dinner, and I served a recipe from one of his cookbooks, a Chilean seafood-and-bread casserole that was a recipe of Leonard Bernstein's wife, Felicia Montealegre. I can't believe I remember her name, much less how to spell it, especially given the fact that her recipe was a gluey, milky, disappointing concoction that practically bankrupted me.

I don't think it was Felicia Montealegre's fault that Craig and I never became friends, but there was no question in my mind after our two meals that we had no future together. Craig was a nice guy, don't get me wrong, but he was so low-key that once I'd gotten to know him, I was almost completely unable to have even imaginary conversations with him while cooking his recipes.

Around this time I met a man named Lee Bailey, and I guess I would have to say that if there were any embers burning in the Craig Claiborne department, they were completely extinguished the moment I met Lee. Lee Bailey was a friend of my friend Liz Smith, who believed that everyone she knew should be friends with everyone else she knew. So one night, she invited us to Lee's house for dinner. Lee lived in the East Forties, in a floor-through below the ground, and what I distinctly remember about it was that it had some sort of straw matting on the walls that probably came from Azuma, and it was just about the most fabulous place I'd ever seen. It was simple, and easy on the eyes, and comfortable, but nothing was expensive, and there was no art to speak of, and no color at all. Everything was beige. As Lee once said, "Be very careful about color."

And then dinner was served. Pork chops, grits, collard greens, and a dish of tiny baked crab apples. It was delicious. It was so straightforward and plain and honest and at the same time so playful. Those crab apples!

They were adorable! The entire evening was mortifying, a revelation, a rebuke in its way to every single thing I had ever bought and every dinner I had ever served. My couch was purple. I owned a collection of brightly painted wooden Mexican animals. I had red plates and a shag rug. My menus were overwrought and overthought. Would Lee Bailey ever in a million years consider cooking the Brazilian national dish? Or Lee Lum's lemon chicken? Certainly not. It was horribly clear that my entire life up to that point had been a mistake.

I immediately got a divorce, gave my ex-husband all the furniture, and began to make a study of Lee Bailey. I bought the chairs he told me to buy, and the round dining room table that seemed to be part of the secret of why Lee's dinner parties were more fun than anyone else's. When Lee opened a store at Henri Bendel, I bought the white plates, seersucker napkins, and wood-handled stainless flatware that were just like his. I bought new furniture, and all of it was beige. I became Lee's love slave, culinarily speaking. Long before he began to write the series of cookbooks that made him well known, he had replaced all my previous imaginary friends in the kitchen, and whenever I cooked dinner and anything threatened to go wrong, I could hear him telling me to calm down, it didn't matter, pour another drink, no one will care. I stopped serving hors d'oeuvres, just like Lee, and as a result, my guests were chewing the wood off the walls before dinner, just like Lee's. I began to osmose from a neurotic cook with a confusing repertory of ethnic dishes to a very relaxed one specializing in faintly Southern food.

The most important thing I learned from Lee was something I call the Rule of Four. Most people serve three things for dinner—some sort of meat, some sort of starch, and some sort of vegetable—but Lee always served four. And the fourth thing was always unexpected, like those crab apples. A casserole of lima beans and pears cooked for hours with brown sugar and molasses. Peaches with cayenne pepper. Sliced tomatoes with honey. Biscuits. Savory bread pudding. Spoon bread. Whatever it was, that fourth thing seemed to have an almost magical effect on the eating process. You never got tired of the food because there was always another taste on the plate that seemed simultaneously to match it and contradict it. You could go from taste to taste; you could mix a little of this with a little of that. And when you finished eating, you always wanted more, so that you could go from taste to taste all over again. At Lee Bailey's you could eat forever. This was important. This was crucial. There's nothing worse than having people to a dinner that they all just polish off and before you know it, they're done eating and dinner is over and it's only ten o'clock and everyone leaves and it's just you and the dishes. (And that was another thing about dinner at Lee's: On top of everything else, he had fewer dishes to wash, because he never ever served a first course or a cheese course; and if he served salad, it just went onto the plate along with everything else.)

And by the way, Lee never served fish, so I never served fish, and I'll tell you why: It's too easy to eat fish. Bim bam boom you're done with a piece of fish, and you're right out the door. When people come to dinner, it should be fun, and part of the fun should be the food. Fish—and I'm sorry to say this but it's true—is no fun. People like to play with their food, and it's virtually impossible to play with fish. If you must have fish, order it at a restaurant.

You might think that having Lee as a real friend might have made it superfluous to have him as an imaginary friend, but you would be wrong. As I conducted my inner conversations with Lee—about what to serve, or what would be the perfect fourth thing to accompany what I was serving—it never occurred to me to pick up the phone and ask him. Lee was much too easygoing; he would just have laughed and said, anything you feel like, honey. He was, in his way, as close to a Zen master as I've ever had, and all of us who fell under his influence began with his style and eventually ended up with our own.

I always secretly wished that Lee would include a recipe of mine in one of his cookbooks—he frequently came to dinner and was always fantastically kind about the food—but he never asked for any of my recipes. He did take a photograph of my backyard for one of his cookbooks, and he used my napkins and plates in the photograph; but of course, I'd bought them at his store in Bendel's, so it didn't really count.

Meanwhile, I got married again, and divorced again. I wrote a thinly disguised novel about the end of my marriage, and it contained recipes. By then, I'd come to realize that no one was ever going to put my recipes into a book, so I'd have to do it myself. I included Lee's recipe for lima beans and pears (unfortunately I left out the brown sugar, and for years people told me they'd tried cooking the recipe and it didn't work), along with my family cook Evelyn's recipe for cheesecake, which I'm fairly sure she got from the back of the Philadelphia cream cheese package. A food writer who wrote about the book carped that the recipes were not particularly original, but it seemed to me she missed the point. The point wasn't about the recipes. The point (I was starting to realize) was about putting it together. The point was about making people feel at home, about finding your own style, whatever it was, and committing to it. The point was about giving up neurosis where food was concerned. The point was about finding a way that food fit into your life.

And after a while, I didn't have to have long internal dialogues with Lee—I'd incorporated what I learned from him and moved on. Four things were not enough; I went to five, and sometimes to six. I liked salad and cheese, so I served salad and cheese. So there were more dishes to wash—so what? On the design front, I left behind beige, and as a result I made all the decorating mistakes that are possible once you do.

And I got married again, by the way. In the course of my third marriage, I have had a series of culinary liaisons. I went through a stretch with Marcella Hazan, a brilliant cookbook author whom I had a somewhat unsatisfactory connection to; with Martha Stewart, whom I worshipped and had long, long imaginary talks with, mostly having to do with my slavish adulation of her; and only last year with Nigella Lawson, whose style of cooking is very similar to mine. I gave up on Nigella when one of her cupcake recipes failed in a big way, but I admire her willingness to use store-bought items in recipes, her lackadaisical qualities when it comes to how things look, and her fondness for home cooking. I especially like making her roast beef dinner, which is very much like my mother's, except for the Yorkshire pudding. My mother didn't serve Yorkshire pudding, although there is a recipe for it on page 61 of *The Gourmet Cookbook*. My mother served potato pancakes instead. I serve Yorkshire pudding *and* potato pancakes. Why not? You only live once.

On Maintenance

I have been trying for weeks to write about maintenance, but it hasn't been easy, and for a simple reason: Maintenance takes up so much of my life that I barely have time to sit down at the computer.

You know what maintenance is, I'm sure. Maintenance is what they mean when they say, "After a certain point, it's just patch patch patch." Maintenance is what you have to do just so you can walk out the door knowing that if you go to the market and bump into a guy who once rejected you, you won't have to hide behind a stack of canned food. I don't mean to be too literal about this. There are a couple of old boyfriends whom I always worry about bumping into, but there's no chance—if I ever did—that I would recognize either of them. On top of which they live in other cities. But the point is that I still think about them every time I'm tempted to leave the house without eyeliner.

There are two types of maintenance, of course. There's Status Quo Maintenance—the things you have to do daily, or weekly, or monthly, just to stay more or less even. And then there's the maintenance you have to do monthly, or yearly, or every couple of years or so— maintenance I think of as Pathetic Attempts to Turn Back the Clock. Into this category fall such things as face-lifts, liposuction, Botox, major dental work, and Removal of Unsightly Things—of varicose veins, for instance, and skin tags, and those irritating little red spots that crop up on your torso after a certain age for no real reason. I'm not going to discuss such issues here. For now, I'm concentrating only on the routine, everyday things required just to keep you from looking like someone who no longer cares.

Hair

We begin, I'm sorry to say, with hair. I'm sorry to say it because the amount of maintenance involving hair is genuinely overwhelming. Sometimes I think that not having to worry about your hair anymore is the secret upside of death.

Tell the truth. Aren't you sick of your hair? Aren't you tired of washing and drying it? I know people who wash their hair every day, and I don't get it. Your hair doesn't need to be washed every day, any more than your black pants have to be dry-cleaned every time you wear them. But no one listens to me. It takes some of my friends an hour a day, seven days a week, just to wash and blow-dry their hair. How they manage to have any sort of life at all is a mystery. I mean, we're talking about 365 hours a year! Nine workweeks! Maybe this made sense when we were young, when the amount of time we spent making ourselves look good bore some correlation to the number of hours we spent having sex (which was, after all, one of the reasons for our spending so much time on grooming). But now that we're older, whom are we kidding?

On top of which, have you tried buying shampoo lately? I mean, good luck to you. Good luck finding anything that says on the label, simply, shampoo. There are shampoos for dry but oily hair and shampoos for coarse but fine hair, and then there are the conditioners and the straighteners and the volumizers. How damaged does your hair have to be to qualify as "damaged"? Why are some shampoos for blondes? Do the blondes get better shampoos than the rest of us? It's totally dizzying, shelf after shelf of products, not one of them capable of doing the job alone.

I deal with all this confusion by taking draconian measures to reduce the amount of time I spend on my hair. I never do my own hair if I can help it, and I try my best to avoid situations that would require me to. Every so often a rich friend asks me if I'd like to go on a trip involving a boat, and all I can think about is the misery of five days in a small cabin struggling with a blow-dryer. And I am never going back to Africa; the last time I was there, in 1972, there were no hairdressers out in the bush, and as far as I was concerned, that was the end of that place.

I'm in awe of the women I know who have magical haircuts that require next to no maintenance. I envy all Asian women—I mean, have you ever seen an Asian woman whose hair looks bad? (No, you haven't. Why is this?) I once read an interview with a well-known actress who said that the thing she was proudest of was that she could blow-dry her own hair, and I was depressed for days afterward. I'm completely inept at blow-drying my own hair. I have the equipment and the products, I assure you. I own blow-dryers with special attachments, and hot rollers and Velcro rollers, and gel and mousse and spray, but my hair looks absolutely awful if I do it myself.

So, twice a week, I go to a beauty salon and have my hair blown dry. It's cheaper by far than psychoanalysis, and much more uplifting. What's more, it takes much less time than washing and drying your own hair every single day, especially if, like me, you live in a large city where a good and reasonably priced hairdresser is just around the corner. Still, at the end of the year, I've spent at least eighty hours just keeping my hair clean and pressed. That's two workweeks. There's no telling what I could be doing with all that time. I could be on eBay, for instance, buying something that will turn out to be worth much less than I bid for it. I could be reading good books. Of course, I could be reading good books while having my hair done—but I don't. I always mean to. I always take one with me when I go to the salon. But instead I end up reading the fashion magazines that are lying around, and I mostly concentrate on articles about cosmetic and surgical procedures. Once I picked up a copy of *Vogue* while having my hair done, and it cost me twenty thousand dollars. But you should see my teeth.

Hair Dye

Many years ago, when Gloria Steinem turned forty, someone complimented her on how remarkably young she looked, and she replied, "This is what forty looks like." It was a great line, and I wish I'd said it. "This is what forty looks like" led, inevitably, to its most significant corollary, "Forty is the new thirty," which led to many other corollaries: "Fifty is the new forty," "Sixty is the new fifty," and even "Restaurants are the new theater," "Focaccia is the new quiche," et cetera.

Anyway, here's the point: There's a reason why forty, fifty, and sixty don't look the way they used to, and it's not because of feminism, or better living through exercise. It's because of hair dye. In the 1950s only 7 percent of American women dyed their hair; today there are parts of Manhattan and Los Angeles where there are no gray-haired women at all. (Once, some years ago, I went to Le Cirque, a well-known New York restaurant, to a lunch in honor of a woman named Jean Harris, who had just that week been released from twelve years in prison for murdering her diet-doctor boyfriend, and she was the only woman in the restaurant with gray hair.)

Hair dye has changed everything, but it almost never gets the credit. It's the most powerful weapon older women have against the youth culture, and because it actually succeeds at stopping the clock (at least where your hair color is concerned), it makes women open to far more drastic procedures (like face-lifts). I can make a case that it's at least partly responsible for the number of women entering (and managing to stay in) the job market in middle and late middle age, as well as for all sorts of fashion trends. For example, it's one of the reasons women don't wear hats anymore, and it's entirely the reason that everyone I know has a closet full of black clothes. Think about it. Fifty years ago, women of a certain age almost never wore black. Black was for widows, specifically for Italian war widows, and even Gloria Steinem might concede that the average Italian war widow made you believe that sixty was the new seventy-five. If you have gray hair, black makes you look not just older but sadder. But black looks great on older women with dark hair—so great, in fact, that even younger women with dark hair now wear black. Even blondes wear black. Even women in L.A. wear black. Most everyone wears black—except for anchorwomen, United States senators, and residents of Texas, and I feel really bad for them. I mean, black makes your life so much simpler. Everything matches black, especially black.

But back to hair dye. I began having my hair dyed about fifteen years ago, and for many years, I was categorized by my colorist as a single-process customer— whatever was being done to me (which I honestly have no idea how to describe) did not involve peroxide and therefore took "only" ninety minutes every six weeks or so. Whenever I complained about how long it took, I was told that I was lucky I wasn't blond. Where hair dye is concerned, being blond is practically a career.

Oh, the poor blondes! They were sitting there at the colorist's when I arrived, and they were still sitting there when I left. Their scalps were sectioned off and dotted with little aluminum-foil packets; they had to sit under hair-dryers; they complained bitterly about their dry and damaged hair and their chronic split ends. I felt superior to them in every way. For the first time in my life, it seemed, there was an advantage to being a brunette.

But then, about a year ago, my colorist gave me several highlights as a present. Highlights, you probably know, are little episodes of blondness that are scattered about your head. They involve peroxide. They extend the length of time involved in hair dying from unbearable to unendurable. As I sat in the chair, waiting for my highlights to sink in, I was bored witless. Hours passed. I couldn't imagine why I had been conned into agreeing to this free trial. I vowed that I would never ever even be tempted to have highlights again, much less to pay money for them. (They are, in addition to being time-consuming, wildly expensive. Naturally.)

But—you will probably not be surprised to hear

this—those highlights were a little like that first sip of brandy Alexander that Lee Remick drank in *Days of Wine and Roses*. I emerged onto Madison Avenue with four tiny, virtually invisible blondish streaks in my hair, and was so thrilled and overwhelmed by the change in my appearance that I honestly thought that when I came home, my husband wouldn't recognize me. As it happened, he didn't even notice I'd done anything to myself. But it didn't matter; from that moment on, I was hooked. As a result, my hair-dying habit now takes at least three hours every six weeks or so, and because my hair colorist is (in her world) only slightly less famous than Hillary Clinton, it costs more per year than my first automobile.

Nails

I want to ask a question: When and how did it happen that you absolutely had to have a manicure? I don't begin to know the answer, but I want to leave the question out there, floating around in the atmosphere, as a reminder that just when you think you know exactly how many things you have to do to yourself where maintenance is concerned, another can just pop up out of nowhere and take a huge bite out of your life.

I spent the first forty-five years of my life never thinking about my nails. Occasionally I filed them with the one lone wretched emery board I owned. (A side note on this subject: One of the compelling mysteries of the world, right up there with the missing socks, is what happens to all the other emery boards in the box of emery boards you bought so that you would have more than just one lone wretched emery board.) Anyway, occasionally I filed my nails, put a little polish on them, and went out into the world. This process took about three minutes, twice a year. (Just kidding. But not by much.) I knew there were women who had manicures on a regular basis, but in my opinion they were indolent women who had nothing better to do. Or they were under the mistaken impression that painted nails were glamorous. They were certainly not women who made their living at a typewriter, the machine that was the sworn enemy of long nails.

And then one day, like mushrooms, a trillion nail places appeared in Manhattan. Suddenly there were more nail places than there were liquor stores, or Kinko's, or opticians, or dry cleaners, or locksmiths, and there are way more of all of those in Manhattan than you can ever understand. Sometimes it seemed there were more nail places in Manhattan than there were nails. Most of these nail places were staffed by young Korean women, all of whom could do a manicure quickly and efficiently and not eat up the clock in any way by feigning the remotest interest in their customers. And they were incredibly cheap—eight or ten dollars at most for a regular manicure.

Soon everyone was getting manicures. If your nails weren't manicured (as opposed to merely clean), you felt ungroomed. You felt ashamed. You felt like sitting on your hands. And so it became necessary to have manicures once a week. Which brings me, alas, to pedicures.

The best thing about a pedicure is that most of the

year, from September to May to be exact, no one except your loved one knows if you have had one. The second best thing about a pedicure is that while you're having your feet done, you have the use of your hands and can easily read or even talk on a cell phone. The third best thing about a pedicure is that when it's over, your feet really do look adorable.

The worst thing about pedicures is that they take way too much time and then, just when you think you're done, you have to wait for your toenails to dry. It takes almost as long for your toenails to dry as it does to have a pedicure. So there you sit, for what seems like eternity, and finally you can't stand waiting one more minute so you gently slip on your sandals and leave and on the way home you absolutely ruin the polish on your big toe and since your big toe is really the only thing anyone notices as far as your feet are concerned, you might as well not have had a pedicure in the first place.

Unwanted Hair

I'm sorry to report that I have a mustache. The truth is, I probably always had a mustache, but for years it was sort of dormant, or incipient, or threatening, in the way a cloudy sky threatens to rain. On a few occasions in my younger years it turned dark and stormy, and when it did, I dealt with it by going to the drugstore and buying a much-too-large jar of something called Jolen creme bleach. (I always tried to buy a *small* jar of Jolen creme bleach, but no one stocks it, for the obvious reason that it costs less than the big jar.) This trip to the store was usually followed, almost immediately, by the discovery of several other barely used, perfectly good much-too-large jars of Jolen creme bleach, which turned out to have been right there all along, under the bathroom sink, where I had just looked for them—I swear I had—and yet didn't see them. Jolen creme bleach turns the mustache on your upper lip to the exact color of Richard Gephardt's hair, which is better than its looking like Frida Kahlo's mustache, but it's still slightly hairier than you mean it to be.

But then, along came menopause. And with it, my mustache changed: It was no longer dormant, incipient, and threatening; it was now just plain there. Fortunately, at the time, I was going to a lovely Russian-born hairdresser named Nina on the Upper West Side of Manhattan who, as it turned out, specialized in something called threading, a fantastic and thrilling method of hair removal she had learned in Russia and which, as far as I can tell, is the only thing the Russians managed to outdo us at in fifty years of the cold war. Threading involves thread—garden-variety sewing thread—a long strand of which is twisted and maneuvered in a sort of cat's cradle configuration so as to remove hair in a way that is quick and painful (although not, I should point out, as painful as, say, labor). The results last about a month.

For a long time, threading seemed like a wonderful and not particularly burdensome addition to my maintenance regime. Nina did my hair twice a week, so it took only five additional minutes for her to thread my mustache—plus, of course, ten additional minutes to thread my eyebrows, not that I needed my eyebrows threaded because my bangs are so long you can't even tell whether I have eyebrows, much less whether they need weeding. But as long as Nina was doing the mustache it seemed to her (and let's face it, to me) that she might as well do the eyebrows too. Having your eyebrows threaded is much more expensive and much more painful (although not, I should point out, as painful as labor), and causes you to sneeze uncontrollably. But that's a small price to pay. In fact, the cost of threading is a small price to pay for the smooth and lovely result.

Unfortunately, though, a couple of years ago, I moved away from the Upper West Side to the Upper East Side of Manhattan, taking my mustache with me but leaving behind Nina and her compelling geographical convenience. So now I must add the travel time (and cab fare) to the cost of threading.

On the other hand, where unwanted hair is concerned, I'm duty-bound to report that I spend considerably less time having myself waxed than I used to because (and you don't see a whole lot of this in those cheerful, idiotic books on menopause) at a certain point, you have less hair in all sorts of places you used to have quite a lot. When I was growing up, I had a friend who was a pioneer in waxing—she first had her legs waxed when she was fifteen, and this was in 1956, when waxing was really practically unknown. She assured me that if I didn't start getting my legs waxed—if I persisted in simply shaving like all the other commoners in the world—the hair would grow in faster and faster and faster and faster and eventually I would look like a bear. This turns out not to be true. You can shave your legs for many years, and they don't really get a whole lot hairier than when they started. And then, at a certain age, they get less hairy. My guess is that by the time I'm eighty, I will be able to handle any offending hair on my legs with two plucks of an eyebrow tweezer.

As for waxing what I like to call my bikini, it has become but a brief episode in what the fashion magazines refer to as my beauty regimen, and owing to my ability to avoid wearing a bathing suit except on rare occasions, I rarely need to do it anymore. (In the old days, however, a bikini wax was not just painful—it was truly as painful as labor. I dealt with the pain by using the breathing exercises I learned in Lamaze classes. I recommend them highly, although not for childbirth, for which they are virtually useless.) I understand that some young women have their pubic hair removed entirely, or shaped, like topiary, into triangles and hearts and the like. I am too old for this, thank God.

Speaking of the pain of labor, which I seem to be, I would like to interject a short, irrelevant note: Why do people always say you forget the pain of labor? I haven't forgotten the pain of labor. Labor hurt. It hurt a lot. The fact that I am not currently in pain and cannot simulate the pain of labor doesn't mean I don't remember it. I am currently not eating a wonderful piece of grilled chicken I once had in Asolo, Italy, in 1982, but I remember it well. It was delicious. I can tell you exactly what it tasted like, and except for the time when I returned to the restaurant six years later and ordered it again (and it turned out, amazingly, to be exactly as wonderful as I remembered), I have never tasted chicken that was crisper, tastier, or juicier. The song has ended, but the melody lingers on, and that goes for the pain of labor— but not in a good way.

Exercise

I would like to be in shape. I have a friend who gets up every morning at 5 a.m. and essentially does a triathlon. I'm not exaggerating. She is Ironwoman. She lifts weights. She runs marathons. She bicycles for hours. Last summer she took swimming lessons, and within a week she was talking about swimming around the island of Manhattan. A few summers ago I decided to do some swimming, and within a week I had swimmer's ear. Have you ever had it? It's torture. Water rattles around in your ear and itches so much that it wakes you up at night, and there's absolutely no way you can scratch it short of plunging your finger into your brain stem. My own theory about Van Gogh is that he cut off his ear because he'd made the mistake of taking up swimming.

In any case, I would like to be in shape. I would. But every time I try to get into shape, something goes wrong and makes it impossible. Let me make this clear: Every time I get into shape, something breaks.

Exercise, as you no doubt know, is a late arrival in

the history of civilization. Until around 1910, people exercised all the time, but they didn't think of it as exercise—they thought of it as life itself. They had to get from one place to the other, usually on foot, and harvest the crop, and wage war, and so on. But then the automobile was invented (not to mention the Sherman tank), and that pretty much led to what we have today—a country full of underexercised (and often overweight) people—and a parallel universe of overexercised (but not necessarily underweight) people. I myself swing between the two universes. I spend time getting into shape; then something breaks, and then I spend time recovering and not being in shape; then I recover and I get into shape; then something new breaks. So far, in the breakage department, I have managed the following: I pulled my lower back doing sit-ups; I threw out my right hip on the treadmill; I got shin splints from jogging; and I entirely destroyed my neck just from rolling over in bed. A few years ago, during a wild and committed period of exercise, I happened to be sent a tape of the movie *Chicago,* and I made the mistake of confusing it with an exercise video. It was, without question, the greatest exercise video I have ever worked out to. I could lift weights forever while watching it. For the first time in my exercising life, I was never bored. I could be Catherine Zeta-Jones, and then I could be Renée Zellweger. I pranced around the apartment waving my five-pound weights here and there and singing "All That Jazz." I have never been happier exercising. But after three weeks, I woke up one morning in horrible pain and discovered

I couldn't move my arms. Millions of dollars in doctor's fees later, it turned out that I had not one but two frozen shoulders, the result (naturally) of lifting too many weights for far too long. It took two years for these frozen shoulders to mostly thaw, and in the meantime, I had pretty much resigned myself to the prospect of never being able to scratch my own back (or zip up a dress). (Not that I wear dresses, but if I did.) But I am now exercising again. I have a trainer. I have my treadmill. I have my TV set over the treadmill. I exercise almost four hours a week, and I would rather be in Philadelphia (although not in labor).

Skin

In my bathroom there are many bottles. There are also many jars. Most of these bottles and jars contain products for the skin, although none of them contain something that is called, merely, "skin cream." Instead they contain face cream, or hand lotion, or body lotion, or foot cream. Remember when we were young? There was only Nivea. Life was so simple. I know in my heart that all these labels on these bottles and jars are whimsical and arbitrary and designed to make vulnerable, pitiable women like me shell out astronomical sums of money for useless products; on the other hand, you will probably never see me using foot cream on my face, just in case.

Here, for example, right next to the sink, is a bottle of something called StriVectin-SD. For exactly five minutes in 2004 StriVectin-SD was thought to be the Fountain of Youth. It instead turned out to be simply skin lotion, a bottle of which cost an arm and a leg. But meanwhile, for one brief shining moment, I believed it was the answer to everything. The woman who sold it to me at the cosmetics counter behaved as if she were slipping me a bottle of aged whiskey during Prohibition. It had just come in, she whispered. It was down in the basement. They couldn't put it out on display, or it would be gone in a twinkling. Only certain customers were being allowed to have it.

Now it sits on the bathroom counter, taking up space, alongside similar testaments to my gullibility—relics of the Retin-A years and the glycolic-acid era and the La Prairie period. One of my good friends once gave me a tiny jar of La Mer cream, which I think cost about a hundred dollars a teaspoon. I still have it, since it is way too valuable to use.

The point is, I have cream for my face. I have lotions for my arms and legs. I have oil for my bath. I have Vaseline for my feet. I cannot begin to tell you how much time I spend rubbing these moisturizers into myself. But I still get pimples on my face and rough patches on my arms and legs. What's more, the skin on my back is so dry that when I take off a black sweater it looks as if it's been in a snowstorm, and the skin on my heels has the consistency of a loofah.

I have no doubt omitted something where maintenance is concerned. The world of maintenance is changing every second, and I may not know about all sorts of things that women my age are up to. (The other day, for instance, I had lunch with a friend who assured me that I hadn't lived until I had tried having some sort of facial that seems to include a mild form of electroshock.)

What I know is that I spend a huge amount of time with my finger in the dike, and that doesn't begin to include all the things I promised not to go into—the pathetic things. I have done any number of things that fall just short of plastic surgery. I even had all the fillings in my mouth replaced with white material, and I swear to God it took six months off my age. From time to time my dermatologist shoots a hypodermic needle full of something called Restylane into my chin, and it sort of fills in the saggy parts. I have had Botox twice, in a wrinkle in my forehead. Once I even had my lips plumped up with a fat injection, but I looked like a Ubangi, so I never did it again.

But the other day, on the street, I passed a homeless woman. I have never understood the feminists who insisted they were terrified of becoming bag ladies, but as I watched this woman shuffle down the street, I finally understood at least my version of it. I don't want to be melodramatic; I am never going to become a bag lady. But I am only about eight hours a week away from looking exactly like that woman on the street—with frizzled flyaway gray hair I would probably have if I stopped dyeing mine; with a potbelly I would definitely develop if I ate just half of what I think about eating every day; with the dirty nails and chapped lips and mustache and bushy eyebrows that would be my destiny if I ever spent two weeks on a desert island.

On Maintenance

Eight hours a week and counting. By the time I reach my seventies, I'm sure it will take at least twice as long. The only consolation I have in any of this is that when I'm very old and virtually unemployable, I will at least have something to do. Assuming, of course, that I haven't spent all my money doing it.

Blind as a Bat

I can't read a word on the map. I know we're on Route 110
heading north, because we just drove past a large sign
that said so. Now we seem to be in Fort Salonga. I'm
sure Fort Salonga is on the map, but I can't find my
reading glasses so I can't read the map. One of the nicest
things about being about to read a map, which I used to
be able to do without reading glasses, is that you're
never really lost if you can find yourself on a map. But
those days are over; we're lost. We hate being lost. I hate
being lost, he hates being lost, and our marriage hates

being lost. On the other hand, I have to admit, we're getting used to it. And because it's my fault (and not my husband's) that I can't find my reading glasses, although it's his fault (and not mine) that there's no magnifying glass in the glove compartment, I say mellow things like "Well, at least we're headed in the right direction." My husband says mellow things too, like "Well, we've never come this way before, so it might be interesting." And he's right. It might be interesting. Except that it's very dark outside, and the only thing I can see clearly is a sign that says we're on Route 110 heading north through Fort Salonga. Wherever that is.

I can't read a word in the telephone book. When I was a young newspaper reporter, I always began by looking in the telephone book. You'd be amazed at how many people were right there, listed, waiting to be found. Years later, I tried to convey this to my children, but they ignored me. It drove me crazy. My children thought that calling Directory Assistance was free, on top of which they always pressed "1" to be connected, for an additional charge of thirty-five cents. This drove me even crazier. Now that I can't read the fine print in the telephone book, I'm forced to call Directory Assistance. I speak to a recording. I miss my relationship with the telephone book. I miss what it stood for. Self-sufficiency. Democracy. The belief that you could find what you were looking for in a place that everyone in the world had access to. Just thinking about the telephone book makes me misty about a world where everyone—or nearly everyone—was in the book, and what's more, I could find them without the assistance of a disembodied recording that doesn't understand a word I'm saying.

I can't read a word on the menu. I can't read a word in the weekly television listings. I can't read a word in the cookbook. I can't do the puzzle. I can't read a word in anything at all unless it's written in extremely large type, the larger the better. The other day, on the computer, I pulled up something I wrote three years ago, and it was written in type so small I can't imagine how I wrote the thing in the first place. I used to write in twelve-point type; now I am up to sixteen and thinking about going to eighteen or even twenty. I'm extremely sad about all this. Mostly I'm sad about just plain reading. When I pass a bookshelf, I like to pick out a book from it and thumb through it. When I see a newspaper on the couch, I like to sit down with it. When the mail arrives, I like to rip it open. Reading is one of the main things I do. Reading is everything. Reading makes me feel I've accomplished something, learned something, become a better person. Reading makes me smarter. Reading gives me something to talk about later on. Reading is the unbelievably healthy way my attention deficit disorder medicates itself. Reading is escape, and the opposite of escape; it's a way to make contact with reality after a day of making things up, and it's a way of making contact with someone else's imagination after a day that's all too real. Reading is grist. Reading is bliss. But my ability to pick something up and read it—which has gone unchecked all my life up until now—is now entirely dependent on the whereabouts of my reading glasses. I look around. Why aren't they in this room? I bought six pair of them last week on sale and sprinkled them throughout the house, yet none of them is visible. Where are they?

I hate that I need reading glasses. I hate that I can't read a word on the map, in the telephone book, on the menu, in the book, or anywhere else without them. And the pill bottle! I forgot to mention the pill bottle. I can't read a word on the pill bottle. Does it say take two every four hours or take four every two hours? Does it say, "Good until 12/08/07" or "Expired. Period. End of Story"? I have no idea what it says, and this is serious. I could die from not being able to read the print on the pill bottle. In fact, the print on the pill bottle is so small I doubt if anyone can read it. I'm not sure I could read it even when I didn't need reading glasses. Although who can remember?

Parenting in Three Stages

Stage One: *The Child Is Born*

I want to begin by saying that when I gave birth to my children, which was not that long ago, there was almost no such thing as parenting as we know it today. There were parents, of course, and there were mothers and fathers (and mothering and fathering), but the concept of parenting was in its very early stages, if it existed at all.

Here's what a parent is: A parent is a person who has

children. Here's what's involved in being a parent: You love your children, you hang out with them from time to time, you throw balls, you read stories, you make sure they know which utensil is the salad fork, you teach them to say please and thank you, you see that they have an occasional haircut, and you ask if they did their homework. Every so often, sentences you never expected to say (because your parents said them to you) fall from your lips, sentences like:

DO YOU HAVE ANY IDEA WHAT THAT COST?

BECAUSE I SAY SO. THAT'S WHY.

I SAID NOW.

STOP THAT THIS MINUTE.

GO TO YOUR ROOM.

I DON'T CARE WHAT JESSICA'S MOTHER LETS HER DO.

A TIARA? YOU WANT A TIARA?

Back in the day when there were merely parents, as opposed to people who were engaged in parenting, being a parent was fairly straightforward. You didn't need a book, and if you owned one, it was by Dr. Spock, a pediatrician, and you rarely looked at it unless your child had

a temperature of 103, or the croup, or both. You understood that your child had a personality. His very own
personality. He was born with it. For a certain period,
this child would live with you and your personality, and
you would do your best to survive each other.

"They never really change," people often said (back
in those days) about babies. This was a somewhat mysti-
fying concept when you first had a baby. Exactly what
was it about the baby that would never change? After
all, it's incredibly difficult to tell what a baby's exact
personality is when it's merely a baby. (I'm using the
word *personality* in the broadest sense, the one that
means "the whole ball of wax.") But eventually the
baby in question began to manifest its personality, and
sure enough, remarkably enough, that personality never
changed. For example, when the police arrived to inform
you that your eight-year-old had just dropped a dozen
eggs from your fifth-floor window onto West End Avenue,
you couldn't help but be reminded of the fourteen-
month-old baby he used to be, who knocked all the string
beans from the high chair to the floor and thought it was
a total riot.

Back in those days—and once again, let me stress
that I am not talking about the nineteenth century here,
it was just a few years ago—no one believed that you
could turn your child into a different human being from
the one he started out being. T. Berry Brazelton, the
pediatrician who supplanted Spock in the 1980s, was a
disciple of Piaget, and his books divided babies into
three types—active, average, and quiet. He never sug-

gested that your quiet baby would ever become an active one, or vice versa. Your baby was your baby, and if he ran you ragged, he ran you ragged; and if he lay in his crib staring happily at his mobile, that was about what you could expect.

All this changed around the time I had children. You can blame the women's movement for it—one of the bedrock tenets of the women's movement was that because so many women were entering the workforce, men and women should share in the raising of children; thus the gender-neutral word *parenting,* and the necessity of elevating child rearing to something more than the endless hours of quantity time it actually consists of. Conversely, you can blame the backlash against the women's movement—lots of women didn't feel like entering into the workforce (or even sharing the raising of children with their husbands), but they felt guilty about this, so they were compelled to elevate full-time parenthood to a sacrament.

In any event, suddenly, one day, there was this thing called parenting. Parenting was serious. Parenting was fierce. Parenting was solemn. *Parenting* was a participle, like *going* and *doing* and *crusading* and *worrying;* it was active, it was energetic, it was unrelenting. Parenting meant playing Mozart CDs while you were pregnant, doing without the epidural, and breast-feeding your child until it was old enough to unbutton your blouse. Parenting began with the assumption that your baby was a lump of clay that could be molded (through hard work, input, and positive reinforcement) into a perfect person who would someday be admitted to the college of your choice. Parenting was not simply about raising a child, it was about transforming a child, force-feeding it like a foie gras goose, altering, modifying, modulating, manipulating, smoothing out, improving. (Interestingly, the culture came to believe in the perfectibility of the child just as it also came to believe in the conflicting theory that virtually everything in human nature was genetic—thus proving that whoever said that a sign of intelligence was the ability to hold two contradictory thoughts simultaneously did not know what he was talking about.)

And by the way, all sorts of additional personnel were required to achieve the transformational effect that was the goal of parenting—baby whisperers, sleep counselors, shrinks, learning therapists, family therapists, speech therapists, tutors—and, if necessary, behavior-altering medication, which, coincidentally or uncoincidentally, was invented at almost the exact moment that parenting came into being.

Parenting carried with it the implicit assumption that any time is quality time if the parent is in attendance. As a result, you were required to be in attendance at the most mundane activities—to watch, cheerlead, and, if necessary, coach, even if this meant throwing your weekend away by driving three hours and twenty minutes in each direction so that you could sit in a dark, hot locker room next door to a gym where your beloved child was going down to resounding defeat in a chess tournament you were not allowed to observe because your mere presence in the room would put unfair pressure on him or her. (The willingness on the part of both parents to be present at any place at any time had the interesting side effect of causing schools to rely on parents to oversee all sorts of events that used to be supervised by trained professionals.)

Parenting meant that whether or not your children understood you, your obligation was to understand them; understanding was the key to everything. If your children believed you understood them, or at least tried to understand them, they wouldn't hate you when they became adolescents; what's more, they would grow up to be happy, well-adjusted adults who would never have to squander their money (or, far more likely, yours) on psychoanalysis or whatever fashion in self-improvement had come along to take its place.

Parenting used entirely different language from just plain parenthood, language you would never write in big capital letters in order to make clear that it had been uttered impulsively or in anger. So it went more or less like this:

I'm sure you didn't mean to break Mommy's antique vase, sweetheart.

We should talk about this.

I know how frustrated and angry you must feel right now.

Why don't you go to your room and take a time-out and come back when you're feeling better.

If you want, I'll call Jessica's mother to see what her reasoning is.

If you finish your homework, we can talk about the tiara.

Stage Two: *The Child Is an Adolescent*

Adolescence comes as a gigantic shock to the modern parent, in large part because it seems so much like the adolescence you yourself went through. Your adolescent is sullen. Your adolescent is angry. Your adolescent is mean. In fact, your adolescent is mean to you.

Your adolescent says words you were not allowed to say while growing up, not that you had even heard of them until you read *The Catcher in the Rye*. Your adolescent is probably smoking marijuana, which you may have smoked too, but not until you were at least eighteen. Your adolescent is undoubtedly having completely inappropriate and meaningless sex, which you didn't have until you were in your twenties, if then. Your adolescent is embarrassed by you and walks ten steps ahead of you so that no one thinks you are remotely acquainted with each other. Your adolescent is ungrateful. You have a vague memory of having been accused by your parents of being ungrateful, but what did you have to be grateful for? Almost nothing. Your parents weren't into parenting. They were merely parents. At least one of them drank like a fish. Whereas you are exemplary. You've devoted years to making your children feel that you care about every single emotion they've ever felt. You've filled every waking second of their lives with cultural activities. The words "I'm bored" have never crossed their lips, because they haven't had time to be bored. Your children have had everything you could give—everything and more, if you count the sneakers. You love them wildly, way more than your parents loved you. And yet they seem to have turned out exactly the way adolescents have always turned out. Only worse. How did this happen? What did you do wrong?

Furthermore, thanks to modern nutritional advances, your adolescent is large, probably larger than you. Your adolescent's weekly allowance is the size of the gross national product of Burkina Faso, a small, poverty-stricken African country neither you nor your adolescent had ever heard of until recently, when you both spent several days working on a social studies report about it.

Your adolescent has changed, but not in any of the ways you'd hoped for when you set about to mold your child. And you have changed too. You have changed from a moderately neurotic, fairly cheerful human being to an irritable, crabby, abused wreck.

But not to worry. There's somewhere you can go for help. You can go to all the therapists and counselors you consulted in the years before your children became adolescents, the therapists and counselors who've put their own children through college and probably law school thanks to your ongoing reliance on them.

Here's what they will say:

- Adolescence is for adolescents, not for parents.
- It was invented to help attached—or overattached— children to separate, in preparation for the inevitable moment when they leave the nest.
- There are things you can do to make life easier for yourself.

This advice will cost you hundreds—or thousands—of dollars, depending on whether you live in a major metropolitan area or a minor one. And it's completely untrue:

- Adolescence is for parents, not adolescents.
- It was invented to help attached—or overattached—*parents* to separate, in preparation for the inevitable moment when their children leave the nest.
- There is almost nothing you can do to make life easier for yourself except wait until it's over.

Incidentally, there's an old joke that was probably invented by someone with adolescent children. Not that I'm good at telling jokes. And if I were, you still wouldn't know how good this joke is, because it takes quite a long time to tell it and requires one of those Yiddish accents people use when telling jokes about old rabbis. But anyway, this married couple goes to see a rabbi. What can I do for you, the rabbi says. We're having a terrible problem, Rabbi, the couple says. We have five children and we all live in a one-room house and we're driving each other crazy. The rabbi says, Move in a sheep. So they move a sheep into the house. A week later they go see the rabbi and tell him that things are worse than ever, plus there's a sheep. Move in a cow, the rabbi says. The next week they go to complain once again, because things are so much worse now that there's a cow. Move in a horse, the rabbi says. The next week the couple goes to see the rabbi to tell him that things are the worst they've ever been. "You're ready for the solution," the rabbi says. "Move the animals out."

Stage Three: *The Child Is Gone*

Oh, the drama of the empty nest. The anxiety. The apprehension. What will life be like? Will the two of you have anything to talk about once your children are gone? Will you have sex now that the presence of your children is no longer an excuse for not having sex?

The day finally comes. Your child goes off to college. You wait for the melancholy. But before it strikes— before it even has time to strike—a shocking thing happens: Your child comes right back. The academic year in American colleges seems to consist of a series of short episodes of classroom attendance interrupted by long vacations. These vacations aren't called "vacations," they're called "breaks" and "reading periods." There are colleges that even have October breaks. Who ever heard of an October break? On a strictly per diem basis, your child could be staying at a nice Paris hotel for about what you're paying in boarding expenses.

In any event, four years quickly pass in this manner. Your children go. Your children come back. Their tuition is raised.

But eventually college ends, and they're gone for good.

The nest is actually empty.

You're still a parent, but your parenting days are over.

Now what?

There must be something you can do.

But there isn't.

There is nothing you can do.

Trust me.

If you find yourself nostalgic for the ongoing, day-to-day activities required of the modern parent, there's a solution: Get a dog. I don't recommend it, because dogs require tremendous commitment, but they definitely give you something to do. Plus they're very loveable and, more important, uncritical. And they can be trained.

But that's about all you can do.

Meanwhile, you have an extra room. Your child's room. Do not under any circumstances leave your child's room as is. Your child's room is not a shrine. It's not going to the Smithsonian. Turn it into a den, a gym, a guest room, or (if you already have all three) a room for wrapping Christmas presents. Do this as soon as possible. Leaving your child's room as is may encourage your child to return. You do not want this.

Meanwhile, every so often, your children come to visit. They are, amazingly, completely charming people. You can't believe you're lucky enough to know them. They make you laugh. They make you proud. You love them madly. They survived you. You survived them. It crosses your mind that on some level, you spent hours and days and months and years without laying a glove on them, but don't dwell. There's no point. It's over.

Except for the worrying.

The worrying is forever.

Moving On

In February 1980, two months after the birth of my second child and the simultaneous end of my marriage, I fell in love. I was looking for a place to live, and one afternoon I walked just ten steps into an apartment on the Upper West Side of Manhattan, and my heart stood still. Head over heels. This was it. At first sight. Eureka. Ten steps in and I said, "I'll take it."

The apartment was huge. It was on the fifth floor of the Apthorp, a famous stone pile on the corner of Broadway and Seventy-ninth Street. The rent was fifteen hundred dollars a month—which was, by Manhattan standards, practically a bargain. Trust me, it was. In addition, I had to pay the previous tenant twenty-four thousand dollars in key money (as it's known in New York City) for the right to move in. I didn't have twenty-four thousand dollars. I went to a bank and borrowed the money. No one in the building could believe that I would pay so much in key money for a rental apartment; it was an astronomical amount. But the apartment had beautiful rooms, most of them painted taxicab yellow (but that could easily be fixed); high ceilings; lots of light; two gorgeous (although non-working) fireplaces; and five, count them, five bedrooms. It seemed to me that if I lived in the building for twenty-four years, the fee would amortize out to only a thousand dollars a year, a very small surcharge—only $2.74 a day, which is less than a cup of cappuccino at Starbucks. Not that there was a Starbucks then. And not that I was planning to live in the Apthorp for twenty-four years. I was planning to live there forever. Till death did us part. So it would probably amortize out to even less. That's how I figured it. (I should point out that I don't normally use the word "amortize" unless I'm trying to prove that something I can't really afford is not just a bargain but practically free. This usually involves dividing the cost of the item I can't afford by the number of years I'm planning to use it, and if that doesn't work, by the number of days or hours or minutes, until I get to a number that is less than the cost of a cup of cappuccino.)

But never mind the money. This, after all, is not a

story about money. It's a story about love. And all stories about love begin with a certain amount of rationalization.

I had never planned to live on the Upper West Side, but after a few weeks, I couldn't imagine living anywhere else, and I began, in my manner, to make a religion out of my neighborhood. This was probably a consequence of my not having any other religion in my life, but never mind. I was a block from H&H Bagels and Zabar's. I was a half block from a subway station. There was an all-night newsstand across the street. On the next corner was La Caridad, the greatest Cuban-Chinese restaurant in the world, or so I told my friends, and I made a religion of it too.

But my true religious zeal focused on the Apthorp itself. I honestly believed that at the lowest moment in my adult life I'd been rescued by a building. All right, I'm being melodramatic, but that's what I believed. I'd left New York City a year earlier to move to Washington, D.C., for what I sincerely thought would be the rest of my life. I'd tried to be cheerful about it. But the horrible reality kept crashing in on me. I would stare out the window of my Washington apartment, which actually had a commanding view of the lions at the National Zoo. The lions at the National Zoo! Oh, the metaphors of captivity that leapt to mind! The lions lived in a large, comfortable space, like me, and had plenty of food, like me. But were they happy? Et cetera. At other times, the old Clairol ad—"If I've only one life to live, let me live it as a blonde"—reverberated through my brain, although my version of it had nothing to do with hair color. If I've only one life to live, I thought, self-pityingly, why am I living it here? But then, of course, I would remember why: I was married, and my husband lived in Washington, and I was in love with him, and we had one baby and another on the way.

When my marriage came to an end, I realized that I would never again have to worry about whether the marginal neighborhood where we lived was ever going to have a cheese store. I would be free to move back to New York City—which was not just the Big Apple but Cheese Central. But I had no hope that I'd ever find a place to rent that I could afford that had room enough for us all.

Whenever you give up your apartment in New York and move to another city, New York turns into the worst version of itself. Someone I know once wisely said that the expression "It's a nice place to visit, but I wouldn't want to live there" is completely wrong where New York is concerned; the opposite is true. New York is a very livable city. But when you move away and become a visitor, the city seems to turn against you. It's much more expensive (because you have to eat all your meals out and pay for a place to sleep) and much more unfriendly. Things change in New York; things change all the time. You don't mind this when you live here; when you live here, it's part of the caffeinated romance of this city that never sleeps. But when you move away, you experience change as a betrayal. You walk up Third Avenue planning to buy a brownie at a bakery you've always been loyal to, and the bakery's gone. Your dry cleaner moves to Florida; your dentist retires; the lady who made the pies on West Fourth Street vanishes; the maître d' at P. J. Clarke's quits, and you realize you're going to have to start from scratch tipping your way into the heart of the cold, chic young woman now at the door. You've turned your back for only a moment, and suddenly everything's different. You were an insider, a native, a subway traveler, a purveyor of inside tips into the good stuff, and now you're just another frequent flyer, stuck in a taxi on the Grand Central Parkway as you wing in and out of La Guardia. Meanwhile, you read that Manhattan rents are going up, they're climbing higher, they've reached the stratosphere. It's seems that the moment you left town, they put a wall around the place, and you will never manage to vault over it and get back into the city again. Finding the apartment in the Apthorp seemed like an urban miracle. I'd found a haven. And the architecture of the building added to the illusion.

The Apthorp, which was built in 1908 by the Astor family, is the size of a full city block. From the street, it's lumpen, middle-European, and solid as a tanker, but its central core is a large courtyard with two beautiful marble fountains and a lovely garden. Enter the courtyard and the city falls away; you find yourself in the embrace of a beautiful sheltered park. There are stone benches where you can sit in the afternoons as your children run merrily around, ride their bicycles, fight with one another, and threaten to fall into the fountain and drown. In the spring there are tulips and azaleas, in summer pale blue hostas and hydrangeas.

Most people who don't live in New York have no idea that New Yorkers have exactly the same sense of neighborhood that supposedly exists in small-town America; in the Apthorp, this sense is magnified because the courtyard provides countless opportunities for its residents to bump into one another and eventually learn one another's names. At Halloween those of us with small children turned the courtyard street lamps into a fantasy of pumpkin-headed ghosts; in December the landlords erected an electric menorah, which coexisted with a Christmas tree covered with twinkle lights.

As it happened, I had several acquaintances who lived in the building, and a few of them became close friends at least in part because we were neighbors. The man I was seeing, whom I eventually married, managed to tip his way to a lease on a top-floor apartment. My sister Delia and her husband moved into the building; she too planned to live there until the day she died. When Delia and I worked together writing movies, it was a simple matter of her coming down from her apartment, crossing the courtyard, and coming up to mine; on rainy days, she could even take an underground route. My friend Rosie O'Donnell took an apartment on the top floor and became so captivated by a doorman named George, who had a big personality, that she booked him onto her talk show. Like most Apthorp doormen, George did not actually open the door—which was, incidentally, a huge, heavy iron gate that you often desperately needed help with—but he did provide a running commentary on everyone who lived in the building, and whenever I came home, he filled me in on the whereabouts of my husband, my boys, my babysitter, my sister, my brother-in-law, and even Rosie, who painted her apartment orange, installed walls of shelves for her extensive collection of Happy Meal toys, feuded with her neighbors about her dogs, fought with the landlord about the fact that her washing machine was somehow irrevocably hooked up to the bathtub drain, and moved out. I was stunned. I couldn't believe that anyone would leave the Apthorp voluntarily. I was never going to leave. They will take me out feet first, I said.

Every so often an ambulance pulled into the courtyard and in fact took a tenant away feet first, and within minutes the landlord would be deluged with inquiries about a possible vacancy, most of them from tenants who had seen the ambulance come in or out (or had heard about it from George) and wanted to upgrade to a larger space.

At the time I moved in, the Apthorp was owned by three elderly persons—although, come to think of it, they were not much older than I am now. One of them was a charming, courtly gentleman, active in all sorts of charities involving Holocaust survivors. He lived long enough to be taken to court for a number of things, none of them including the crime I happen to know he was guilty of, which was lining his pockets with cash payoffs made by people who were either moving in or out of the building. I was very fond of him and his sporty red

Porsche, which he drove right up to the day he was taken to the hospital. There he took his last kickback, from neighbors of mine, and died. The kickback, incidentally, was $50,000—part of the $285,000 in key money my neighbors had charged a new tenant for the right to take over their lease. That's right. Someone paid $285,000 in key money to move into the Apthorp. How was this possible? What was the thinking? Actually I could guess: The thinking was that over fifty-six years, the $285,000 would amortize out to four cappuccinos a day. Grande cappuccinos. *Mucho* grande cappuccinos.

I lived in the Apthorp in a state of giddy delirium for about ten years. The tap water in the bathtub often ran brown, there was probably asbestos in the radiators, and the exterior of the building was encrusted with soot. Also, there were mice. Who cared? My rent slowly inched up—the rent-stabilization law gave landlords the right to raise the rent approximately 8 percent every two years—but the apartment was still a bargain. By this time the real estate boom had begun in New York, and the newspapers were full of shocking articles about escalating rents; there were one-room apartments in Manhattan renting for two thousand dollars a month. I was paying the same amount for eight rooms. I felt like a genius.

Meanwhile, there were unhappy tenants in the building, suing the landlord over various grievances; I couldn't imagine why. What did they want? Service? A paint job every so often? The willing replacement of a broken appliance? There were residents who even complained about the fact that the building didn't allow your Chinese food to be brought up to your apartment. So what? Every time I walked into the courtyard at the end of a day, I fell in love all over again.

My feelings were summed up perfectly by a policeman who turned up one night to handle an altercation on my floor. My next-door neighbor was a kind and pleasant professor, the sort of man who would not hurt a flea; his son often left his bicycle in the vestibule outside our apartment. Our neighbor down the hall, an accountant, became angry about the professor's son's bicycle, which he apparently thought was an eyesore, which it probably was. One afternoon he decided to put it directly in front of the professor's door, blocking it. The professor found the bike there and returned it to its spot in the hallway. The accountant put it back, once again blocking the professor's door. There was quite a lot of noisy crashing about while all this was going on, and it got my attention; as a result, I was lurking at my front door peeking out into the vestibule when the final chapter of the drama occurred.

The professor had just put the bicycle back out in the hall, and he too was waiting inside his front door hoping to catch the accountant in the act of once again moving it. Both of us stood there idiotically looking through the sheer curtains on our glass-paneled front doors. Sure enough, the accountant came down the hall and moved the bicycle to block the professor's door. At that moment, the professor flung his door open and began shouting at the accountant, whom, incidentally, he towered over. Within seconds, he lost it completely and slugged the accountant. It was incredibly exciting. The accountant called the police. The police arrived in short order. Since I, owing to my nosiness, had been a witness to the incident, I invited myself to the meeting with the police and my two neighbors. The meeting took place in the professor's rent-stabilized apartment, which had even more bedrooms than mine. Everyone told his version of events, and then I told mine. I have to say mine was the best version, since it included a short, extremely insightful and probably completely irrelevant digression about the impatience childless people have for people with children (and bicycles). You had to be there. Anyway, when we were all finished, the policeman shook his head and stood up. "Why can't you people get along?" he said as he headed for the door. "I would kill to live in this building."

Eventually, I began to have a recurring dream about the Apthorp—although to be accurate, it was a recurring nightmare: I dreamed I had accidentally moved out of the building, realized it was the worst mistake of my life, and couldn't get my lease back. I have had enough psychoanalysis to know not to take such dreams literally, but it's nonetheless amazing to me that when my unconscious mind searched for a symbol of what I would most hate to lose, it came up with my apartment.

Around 1990, rumors began to spread that there was about to be a change in the law: Under certain circumstances, rent stabilization could be abolished, and landlords would be able to raise the rent to something known as fair market value. I refused to pay any attention. My neighbors were obsessed with what might happen; they suggested that our rents might be raised to eight or ten thousand dollars a month. I thought they were being unbelievably neurotic. Rent stabilization was an indelible part of New York life, like Gray's Papaya. It would never be tampered with. I was willing to concede (well, not too willing) that under certain circumstances there might be some justice in the new law; I could understand that you could make a case (a weak case) that people like me had been getting away with a form of subsidized housing for years; I could see (dimly) that the landlords were entitled to *something*. But if our rents were raised, I was sure the hike would be a reasonable one. After all, the tenants in the building were a family. The landlords understood that. They would never do anything so unreasonable as to double or triple our rents. This moment of idiotic innocence on my part was comparable to the moment—early in all love stories that end badly—when a wife first discovers the faintest whiff of another woman's perfume on her husband's shirt, decides it's nothing, and goes blithely about her business. I went blithely about my business. And then the building hired a manager named Barbara Ross.

Miss Ross was a small, frightening woman with pale white skin, bright red lips, and a huge, jet-black beehive of hair on top of her head. The beehive was so outsized and bizarre that it reminded me of the 1950s urban legend about the woman who teased her hair so much that cockroaches moved in. Her voice dripped honey, which made her even more terrifying. She was either forty years old or seventy, no one knew. She wore pink silk shantung suits with gigantic shoulder pads. She lurked everywhere. She lived in New Jersey, but she spent Thursday nights in the building office, and rumor had it that she snuck around in her bare feet, trying to catch the elevator operators napping. She issued memos discouraging children from playing ball in the courtyard. She repaved the courtyard and covered the cobblestones with tar. She had a way of coming upon you in the hallway and making you feel guilty even if you were entirely innocent. She was, in short, a character from a nightmare—so much so that she instantly became a running character in mine: I began to dream that I had accidentally moved out of the Apthorp, realized it was the worst mistake of my life, and couldn't get my lease back *because of Miss Ross.*

Meanwhile, the unthinkable happened. The state legislature passed a luxury decontrol law stating that any tenant whose rent was more than $2,500 a month and who earned more than $250,000 a year would automatically be removed from rent stabilization. I couldn't believe it. I was stunned. I could understand the new law applying to *new* tenants, but how on earth could it apply it to those of us who had lived in the building for years under the implicit bargain involved in rent stabilization? I had never even gotten a paint job from the

building, I'd never even asked for one, and now the landlords were about to treat me as if I were living in a luxury apartment. It was practically unconstitutional! It
was totally unfair! It was completely unjust! It was
wrong! It was also, of course, not remotely compelling to
anyone in the outside world. I made a very decent living.
I was going to have my rent raised. What's more, I was
going to be the very first person in the building to
undergo the experience. And no one cared. Even I
wouldn't have cared if I hadn't been me. On the other
hand, I wasn't exactly me. I was in love. I was a true
believer, just like one of those French villagers in the
Middle Ages who come to believe they've seen the tears
of Saint Cecilia on a scrap of oilcloth; I was a character in a story about mass delusion and the madness of
crowds. I was, in short, completely nuts.

And so I went to see Miss Ross. As I recall, I gave a
tender speech about my love for the building. It was
incredibly moving, if not to her. She informed me that
my rent was going to be tripled. We negotiated. She
dropped the price. She dropped it just enough for me to
believe that I had managed a small victory. How much
did she drop it to? I can't possibly tell you. I'm too embarrassed to type the number. Even if I assured you that in
the context of New York rents it wasn't even that outra-
geous, you'd never believe me. The point is, I agreed to
pay it. I signed a new lease.

I signed because I had enough money to pay rent but
not nearly enough to buy an apartment nearly as nice
anywhere in the city.

I signed because my accountant was able, in that

compelling way accountants have, to convince me that the money I would pay in rent was less than I would pay in monthly maintenance plus mortgage interest on a co-op apartment.

I signed because I was, as you already know, an expert in rationalization, and I convinced myself that there were huge savings involved in my staying in the building. The cost of moving, for instance. The cost of new telephone service. The cost of the postage required to notify my friends that I would be living at a new address. The cost of furniture, in case I needed new furniture for the apartment I hadn't found and wasn't moving into. The hours and days and possibly even weeks of my time that would be wasted trying to reach the cable company—during which time I might instead write a great novel and earn a small fortune that would more than pay for the rent increase.

But as I said, this isn't a story about money. This is a story about love. I signed the lease because I wasn't ready to get a divorce—from my building.

Many years ago, when I was in analysis, my therapist used to say, "Love is homesickness." What she meant was that you tend to fall in love with someone who reminds you of one of your parents. This, of course, is one of those things that analysts always say even though it really isn't true. Just about anyone on the planet is capable of reminding you of something about one of your parents, even if it's only a dimple. But I don't mean to digress. The point I want to make is that love may or may not be homesickness, but homesickness is most definitely love. My apartment in the Apthorp was really the only space my children and I had ever lived in together. Since the day we moved in we'd never even locked the door. It was the place where Max got his head stuck in a cake pan and Jacob learned to tie his shoelaces. Nick and I were married there, in front of the nonworking living room fireplace. It was a symbol of family. It was an emblem of the moment in my life when my luck changed. It was part of my identity, or at least part of my wishful thinking about my identity. Because it was on the unfashionable West Side, just living there made me feel virtuous and brainy. Because it was a rental, it made me feel unpretentious. Because it was shabby, it made me feel chic. In short, it was home in a profound, probably narcissistic, and I suspect all-too-typical way, and it seemed to me no place on earth would ever feel the same.

The whammies began to mount up. A mysterious dead body was found on the roof of the building. One of the apartments caught fire. An apartment on the eleventh floor was robbed and the housekeeper in it was assaulted.

And then the truly shocking things began to happen. The landlords cleaned the building! The landlords, who had basically done nothing to the building since we'd moved in, sandblasted the soot from the exterior, replaced pipes, redid the elevators, and painted the elevator and lobby ceilings gold. They dressed the building employees in braided uniforms with epaulets; the staff began to look like a Hispanic version of Sergeant Pepper's Lonely Hearts Club Band. The senior landlord, a man in his nineties named Nason Gordon, removed the mailbox from the building entrance and replaced it with a large marble statue of a naked woman, which the tenants instantly christened Our Lady of the Apthorp. He dotted the courtyard with horrible white stucco urns and statues of lions. The tenants experienced all of this—every last bit—as acts of hostility. The improvements were clearly being made for one reason and one reason alone—to raise our rents. Which was true; every time the landlords spent money on the building, they trotted off to the Rent Stabilization Board and asked for rent increases based on their expenditures. As a result, more and more tenants lurched toward luxury decontrol and a state of absolute panic. The fear was exacerbated by the fact that the new law made it possible for landlords to be utterly capricious about the rent rises. After all, what was fair market value for an eight-room apartment in a city where there were almost no eight-room apartments for rent?

The 1990s were cresting, and there was a huge amount of money out there in the streets of New York. Empty apartments in the Apthorp were renovated, Miss Ross picked out garish chandeliers for them, and rich tenants moved in. One of the new tenants was actually paying twenty-four thousand dollars a month in rent. Twenty-four thousand dollars a month—and you still couldn't get the doorman to open the gate or the Chinese food delivered to you. Rich men getting divorces moved in. Movie stars came and went.

The courtyard, once an idyllic spot full of happy laughing children, was suddenly crowded with idling limousines waiting for the new tenants to be spirited away to their fabulous midtown careers. Angry tenants waved petitions and legal papers and spread rumors of further impending rent rises.

My lease expired again, and Miss Ross called to tell me that my rent was being raised. The landlords were willing to give me a three-year lease—ten thousand dollars a month the first year, eleven thousand the second, twelve thousand the third. My rent had effectively been raised 400 percent in three years.

And just like that, I fell out of love. Twelve thousand dollars a month is a lot of cappuccino. And guess what? I don't drink cappuccino. I never have. I called a real estate broker and began to look at apartments. Unrequited love's a bore, as Lorenz Hart once wrote. It had taken me significantly longer to come to that realization in the area of real estate than it ever had in the area of marriage, but I was finally, irrevocably there. Since I was involved in a one-sided love affair with the building, falling out of love was fairly uncomplicated. My children were grown and unable to voice the sorts of objections they had put forth during early exploratory conversations on the topic of moving, when they implored me not to move out of the only home they'd ever known. My husband was up for anything. My sister was already on the street, looking for a new place—my sister who'd been quoted in *The New York Times* talking about the "heart and soul" of the Apthorp—was out there, cold-eyed, unsentimental, and threatening to move downtown. I called my accountant, who explained to me (as carefully as he had explained to me only a few years earlier that it made more sense to rent than to buy) that it made more sense to buy than to rent.

So we prepared to move. We threw away whole pieces of our lives: the Care Bears, the wire shelving in the basement storage room, the boxes full of bank statements, the posters we hung on the walls when we were young, the stereo speakers that no longer worked, the first computer we ever bought, the snowboard, the surfboard, the drum kit, the Portafiles full of documents relating to movies never made. Boxes of clothing went to charity. Boxes of books went to libraries in homeless shelters. We felt cleansed. We'd gotten back to basics. We'd been forced to confront what we'd outgrown, what we'd no longer need, who we were. We'd Taken Stock. It was as if we'd died but got to sort through our things; it was as if we'd been reborn and were now able to start accumulating things all over again.

Our new place was considerably smaller than our apartment in the Apthorp. It was on the Upper East Side, a neighborhood that on some level I had spent more than twenty years thinking of as the enemy of everything I held dear. It was nowhere near a Cuban-Chinese restaurant. But the fireplace worked, the door-man opened the door, and the Chinese food was delivered to your apartment. Within hours of moving in, I was home. I was astonished. I was amazed. Most of all, I was mortified. I hadn't been so mortified since the end of my second marriage, and a great many of the things that went through my head apropos of that marriage went through my head now: Why hadn't I left at the first whiff of the other woman's perfume? Why hadn't I realized how much of what I thought of as love was simply my own highly developed gift for making lemonade? What failure of imagination had caused me to forget that life was full of other possibilities, including the possibility that eventually I would fall in love again?

On the other hand, I am never going to dream about this new apartment of mine.

At least I haven't so far.

And I am never going to feel romantic about the neighborhood—although I have to say that it's much more appealing than I would have guessed. What's more, it turns out to possess many of the things that made the Apthorp so wildly compelling—proximity to an all-night newsstand, an all-night Korean grocery, and even a twenty-four-hour Kinko's. It's spring now, and I can see out the window that the pear trees are in bloom, and they're just beautiful . . . and by the way, shopping for food is every bit as good on this side of town as it was on the West Side, it's much closer to the airport, the subway is better, and I'll tell you something else I've noticed about the East Side: It's sunnier, it really is, I don't know why, the light is just much lighter on the East Side of town than the West. What's more, it's definitely warmer over here in winter because it's farther from the frigid blasts of wind coming off the Hudson River. And it's much closer to all my doctors' offices, which is something you have to think about at my age, I'm sorry to say. A block from here is a place that sells the most heavenly Greek yogurt, and a block in another direction is a restaurant I could honestly eat in every night, that's how good it is.

But it's not love. It's just where I live.

Me and JFK:
Now It Can Be Told

JFK intern admits all

John F. Kennedy's intern admitted to the *Daily News* yesterday: "I am the Mimi."

Marion (Mimi) Fahnestock, now 60, called it a huge weight off her shoulders to finally reveal her affair with the dashing young president four decades ago. "The gift for me is that this allowed me to tell my two married daughters a secret that I've been holding for 41 years," she said. "It's a huge relief. And now I will have no further comment on this subject. I request that the media respect my privacy and that of my family."

I was an intern in the JFK White House. I was. This is not one of those humor pieces where the writer pretends to some experience currently in the news in order to make an "amusing" point. It was 1961, and I was hired by Pierre Salinger to work in the White House press office, the very same place where Mimi Fahnestock was to work the following year. And now that Mimi Fahnestock has been forced to come forward and admit that she had an affair with JFK, I might as well tell my story too.

I notice that all the articles about poor Mimi quote another woman in the press office, Barbara Gamarekian, who fingered Fahnestock in the oral history archives at the Kennedy Library. Gamarekian cattily pointed out, according to the newspapers, that Mimi "couldn't type." Well, all I can say to that is: Ha. In fact: Double ha. There were, when I worked there, six women in Pierre Salinger's office. One of them was called Faddle (her best friend, Fiddle, worked for Kennedy), and her entire job, as far as I could tell, was autographing Pierre Salinger's photographs. Fiddle's job was autographing Kennedy's. Typing was not a skill that anyone seemed to need, and it certainly wasn't necessary for interns like me (and Mimi, dare I say), because THERE WAS NO DESK FOR AN INTERN TO SIT AT AND THEREFORE NO TYPEWRITER TO TYPE ON.

Yes, I am still bitter about it! Because there I was, not just the only young woman in the White House who was unable to afford an endless succession of A-line sleeveless linen dresses just like Jackie's, but also the only person in the press office with nowhere to sit. And then, as now, I could type one hundred words a minute. Every eight-hour day there were theoretically forty-eight thousand words that weren't being typed because I DIDN'T HAVE A DESK.

Also, I had a really bad permanent wave. This is an important fact for later in the story, when things heat up.

I met the president within minutes of going to "work" in the White House. My first morning there, he flew to Annapolis to give the commencement address, and Salinger invited me to come along with the press pool in the press helicopter. When I got back to the White House, Pierre took me in to meet Kennedy. He was the handsomest man I had ever seen. I don't remember the details of our conversation, but perhaps they are included in Salinger's reminiscences in the Kennedy Library. Someday I will look them up. What I do remember is that the meeting was short, perhaps ten or fifteen seconds. After it, I went back to the press office and discovered what you, reader, already know: that there was no place for me to sit.

So I spent my summer internship lurking in the hall near the file cabinet. I read most of the things that were in the file cabinet, including some interesting memos that were marked "Top Secret" and "Eyes Only." Right next to the file cabinet was the men's room, and one day the speaker of the House, Sam Rayburn, inadvertently locked himself into it. Had I not been nearby, he might be there still.

From time to time I went into the Oval Office and watched the president be photographed with various foreign leaders. Sometimes, I am pretty sure, he noticed me watching him.

Which brings me to my crucial encounter with JFK, the one that no one at the Kennedy Library has come to ask me about. It was a Friday afternoon, and because I had nowhere to sit (see above) and nothing to do (ditto), I decided to go out and watch the president leave by helicopter for a weekend in Hyannis Port. It was a beautiful day, and I stood out under the portico overlooking the Rose Garden, just outside the Oval Office. The helicopter landed. The noise was deafening. The wind from the chopper blades was blowing hard (although my permanent wave kept my hair glued tightly to my head). And then suddenly, instead of coming out of the living quarters, the president emerged from his office and walked right past me to get to the helicopter. He turned. He saw me. He recognized me. The noise was deafening but he spoke to me. I couldn't hear a thing, but I could read his lips, and I'm pretty sure what he said was "How are you coming along?" But I wasn't positive. So I replied as best I could. "What?" I said.

And that was it. He turned and went off to the helicopter, and I went back to standing around the White House until the summer was over. I never saw him again.

Now that I have read the articles about Mimi Fahnestock, it has become horribly clear to me that I am probably the only young woman who ever worked in the

Kennedy White House that the president did not make a pass at. Perhaps it was my permanent wave, which was a truly unfortunate mistake. Perhaps it was my wardrobe, which mostly consisted of multicolored Dynel dresses that looked like distilled Velveeta cheese. Perhaps it's because I'm Jewish. Don't laugh; think about it—think about that long, long list of women JFK slept with. Were any of them Jewish? I don't think so.

On the other hand, perhaps nothing happened between us simply because JFK somehow sensed that discretion was not my middle name. I mean, I assure you that if anything had gone on between the two of us, you would not have had to wait this long to find it out.

Anyway, that's my story. I might as well go public with it, although I have told it to pretty much everyone I have ever met in the last forty-two years. And now, like Mimi Fahnestock, I will have no further comment on this subject. I request that the media respect my privacy and that of my family.

Me and Bill:
The End of Love

I broke up with Bill a long time ago. It's always hard to remember love—years pass and you say to yourself, Was I really in love, or was I just kidding myself? Was I really in love, or was I just pretending he was the man of my dreams? Was I really in love, or was I just desperate? But when it came to Bill, I'm pretty sure it was the real deal. I loved the guy.

As for Bill, I have to be honest: He did not love me. In fact, I never even crossed his mind. Not once. But in the beginning that didn't stop me. I loved him, I believed in him, and I didn't even think he was a liar. Of course, I knew he'd lied about his thing with Gennifer, but at the time I believed that lies of that sort didn't count. How stupid was that?

Anyway, I fell out of love with Bill early in the game—over gays in the military. That was in 1993, after he was inaugurated, and at that moment my heart turned to stone. People use that expression and mean it metaphorically, but if your heart can turn to stone and not have it be metaphorical, that's how stony my heart was where Bill was concerned. I'd had faith in him. I'd been positive he'd never back down. How could he? But then he did, he backed down just like that. He turned out to be just like the others. So that was it. Goodbye, big guy. I'm out of here. Don't even think about calling. And by the way, if your phone rings and your wife answers and the caller hangs up, don't think it's me because it's not.

By the time Bill got involved with Monica, you'd have thought I was past being hurt by him. You'd have thought I'd have shrugged and said I told you so, you can't trust the guy as far as you can spit. But much to my surprise, Bill broke my heart all over again. I couldn't believe how betrayed I felt. He'd had it all, he'd had everything, and he'd thrown it away. And here's the thing: It wasn't his to throw away. It was ours. We'd given it to him, and he'd squandered it.

Years passed. I'd sit around with friends at dinner talking about How We Got Here and Whose Fault Was It? Was it Nader's fault? Or Gore's? Or Scalia's? Even

Monica got onto the list, because after all, she delivered the pizza, and that pizza was truly the beginning of the end. Most of my friends had a hard time narrowing it down to a choice, but not me; only one person was at fault, and it was Bill. I drew a straight line from that pizza to the war. The way I saw it, if Bill had behaved, Al would have been elected, and thousands and thousands of people would be alive today who are instead dead.

I bring all this up because I bumped into Bill the other day. I was watching a Sunday news program, and there he was. I have to say, he looked good. And he was succinct, none of that wordy blah-blah thing that used to drive me nuts. He'd invited a whole bunch of people to a conference in New York, and they'd spent the week talking about global warming, and poverty, and all sorts of obscure places he knows a huge amount about.

When Bill described the conference, it was riveting. I could see how much he cared; and of course, I could see how smart he was. It was so refreshing. It was practically moving. To my amazement, I could even see why I'd loved the guy in the first place. It made me sadder than I can say. It's much easier to get over someone if you can delude yourself into thinking you never really cared that much.

Then, later in the week, I was reading about Bill's conference, and I came upon something that made me think, for just a moment, that Bill might even want me back. "I've reached an age now where it doesn't matter whatever happens to me," he said. "I just don't want anyone to die before their time anymore." It almost really got to me. But then I came to my senses. And instead I just wanted to pick up the phone and call him and say, if you genuinely believe that, you hypocrite, why don't you stand up and take a position against this war?

But I'm not calling. I haven't called in years and I'm not starting now.

Where I Live

1. I live in New York City. I could never live anywhere else. The events of September 11 forced me to confront the fact that no matter what, I live here and always will. One of my favorite things about New York is that you can pick up the phone and order anything and someone will deliver it to you. Once I lived for a year in another city, and almost every waking hour of my life was spent going to stores, buying things, loading them into the car, bringing them home, unloading them, and carrying them into the house. How anyone gets anything done in these places is a mystery to me.

2.   I live in an apartment. I could never live anywhere
but in an apartment. I love apartments because I lose
everything. Apartments are horizontal, so it's much easier to find the things I lose—such as my glasses, gloves,
wallet, lipstick, book, magazine, cell phone, and credit
card. The other day I actually lost a piece of cheese in my
apartment. Also, apartment buildings have doormen, a
convenience if you're having things delivered to you,
which I often am, sometimes to replace the things I can't
find.

3.   I live in my neighborhood. My neighborhood consists
of the dry cleaner, the subway stop, the pharmacist, the
supermarket, the cash machine, the deli, the beauty
salon, the nail place, the newsstand, and the place where
I go for lunch. All this is within two blocks of my house.
Which is another thing I love about life in New York:
Everything is right there. If you forgot to buy parsley, it
takes only a couple of minutes to run out and get it. This
is good, because I often forget to buy parsley.

4.   I live at my desk. It's eighty-four inches long and
twenty-eight inches high, a custom height to avoid
computer-related ailments like carpal tunnel syndrome.
My desk is painted white. My computer is a Power Mac
G4, and I spend most of the day and half the night at it.
Only yesterday, while surfing the net, I discovered that
there's an expression for what I am—a mouse potato. It
means someone who's as connected to her computer as
couch potatoes are to their television sets. My favorite
thing about my desk is that it has a huge drawer on the

lower left side that contains a monster wastebasket. I probably didn't invent the concept of building a wastebasket into a desk, but I might have, and whether I did or not, it feels like a breakthrough. As a result, there's no ugly wastebasket on view, taking up floor space and full of horrible, messy crumpled pieces of paper and old tea bags. I highly recommend building a wastebasket into a desk, and I have every hope that just by writing about it here, it will catch on, big-time, and become the thing I'm remembered for. My desk is a mess. Many of the things I'm missing are buried somewhere on it, although some are in my wastebasket, where I have mistakenly thrown them.

5.   And of course, I live in the kitchen. Sometimes I go there to eat, sometimes I go there to figure out what I'm going to eat the next time I eat, and sometimes I go there for a little exercise. I'm not exaggerating when I say that I walk into my kitchen about a hundred times a day. I think I'll go there right now to finish the apple I started eating exactly one minute ago. I hope it's still there.

The Story of My Life
in 3,500 Words or Less

If I can just get back to New York, I'll be fine

I'm five years old. We've just moved from New York to Los Angeles, and I'm outside, at a playground, at my new school on Doheny Drive in Beverly Hills. The sunlight dapples through the trees, and happy laughing blond children surround me. All I can think is, What am I doing here?

.   .   .

What my mother said

My mother says these words at least five hundred times in the course of my growing up: "Everything is copy."

She also says, "Never ever buy a red coat."

What my teacher said

My high school journalism teacher, whose name is Charles O. Simms, is teaching us to write a lead—the first sentence or paragraph of a newspaper story. He writes the words "Who What Where When Why and How" on the blackboard. Then he dictates a set of facts to us that goes something like this: "Kenneth L. Peters, the principal of Beverly Hills High School, announced today that the faculty of the high school will travel to Sacramento on Thursday for a colloquium in new teaching methods. Speaking there will be anthropologist Margaret Mead and Robert Maynard Hutchins, the president of the University of Chicago." We all sit at our typewriters and write a lead, most of us inverting the set of facts so that they read something like this, "Anthropologist Margaret Mead and University of Chicago President Robert Maynard Hutchins will address the faculty Thursday in Sacramento at a colloquium on new teaching methods, the principal of the high school Kenneth L. Peters announced today." We turn in our leads. We're very proud. Mr. Simms looks at what we've done and then tosses everything into the garbage. He says: "The

lead to the story is 'There will be no school Thursday.' "
An electric lightbulb turns itself on in the balloon over
my head. I decide at this moment that I am going to be a
journalist. A few months later I enter a citywide contest
to write an essay in fifty words or less on why I want to
be a journalist. I win first prize, two tickets to the world
premiere of a Doris Day movie.

I swear to God Janice Glabman
will never laugh at me again

I go off to college. I weigh 106 pounds. I come back
from college three months later. I weigh 126 pounds. I
was once thin and shapeless. Now I am fat and, ironi-
cally, equally shapeless. Nothing fits, except for my wool
plaid Pendleton pleated skirt, which makes me look
even fatter. It's tragic. My father takes one look at me as
I get off the plane and says to my mother, "Well, maybe
someone will marry her for her personality."

I go back to college. I stay fat. There's a machine in
the dormitory cafeteria called The Cow, and when you
press a nozzle, out comes the coldest, most delicious milk
you've ever tasted. Also there are sticky buns and
popovers and scones. I have never been exposed to such
wonders. I love them. I have seconds. I have thirds.
There's butter everywhere you look, and of course, that
cold, delicious milk. We're not talking low-fat milk, my
friends. This was so long ago no one even knew about
low-fat milk.

Anyway, months pass. I come home for the summer.

I'm as fat as ever. None of my clothes fit. I already said that, and it's still true. And because it's summer, I can't even wear my wool plaid Pendleton pleated skirt. So I go over to my friend Janice Glabman's to borrow some clothes from her. Janice has always been overweight. I try on a pair of her pants. They're too small. They're way too small. I can't even zip them up. Janice laughs at me. These are Janice's exact words: "Ha ha ha ha ha." The next day I go on a diet. In six months my weight drops back to 106. I have been on a diet ever since.

I have not seen Janice in more than forty years, but if I do see her, I'm ready. I'm thin. Although I now weigh 126 pounds, the exact amount I weighed when I came home from college having become a butterball. I can't explain this.

I am not going to marry Stanley J. Fleck

I'm working as a summer intern in the Kennedy White House, and I'm engaged to be married to a young lawyer named Stanley J. Fleck. Everyone I know is engaged to be married. My fiancé is visiting me in Washington, and I give him a tour of the White House, which I have a pass to roam freely. I show him the Red Room. I show him the Blue Room. I show him the beautiful portrait of Grace Coolidge. I show him the Rose Garden. At the end of the tour, he says, "No wife of mine is ever going to work at a place like this."

· · ·

Sunday in the park

I'm in a rowboat on the lake in Central Park. Fortunately I'm not rowing the boat. I'm still in college, but soon I won't be, soon I'll be living here, in New York City. I look up at all the buildings surrounding the park, and it crosses my mind that except for the man rowing the boat, I don't know anyone in New York City. And I barely know the man in the boat. I wonder if I'm going to end up being one of those people you read about in newspapers, who lives in New York and never meets anyone and eventually dies and no one even notices until days later, when the smell drifts out into the hallway. I vow that someday I will know someone in New York City.

I'm going to be a newspaper reporter forever

It's 1963. I've written a piece for a parody of the *New York Post* during a long newspaper strike. The editors of the *Post* are upset about the parody, but the publisher of the *Post* is amused. "If they can parody the *Post,* they can write for it," she says. "Hire them." When the strike ends, I'm given a one-week tryout at the *Post.* The city room is dusty, dingy, and dark. The desks are dilapidated and falling apart. It smells terrible. There aren't enough phones. The city editor sends me to the Coney Island aquarium to cover the story of two hooded seals who've been brought together to mate but have refused to have anything to do with each other. I write a story. I think it's funny. I turn it in. I hear laughter from the city

101

desk. They think it's funny too. I am hired permanently. I have never been happier. I have achieved my life's ambition, and I am twenty-two years old.

I may not be a newspaper reporter forever

One night I go to a bar near the *Post* with one of my fellow reporters and the managing editor. It's been raining. After quite a few drinks, the managing editor invites us to his home in Brooklyn Heights. When we get there, he tells me to stand on the stoop in front of the house. There's an awning over one of the windows. As I step into position, he lowers the awning, and about ten gallons of water drench me from head to toe. He thinks this is hilarious.

My life changes

I write a magazine article about having small breasts. I am now a writer.

What my mother said (2)

I now believe that what my mother meant when she said "Everything is copy" is this: When you slip on a banana peel, people laugh at you; but when you tell people you slipped on a banana peel, it's your laugh. So you become the hero rather than the victim of the joke.

I think that's what she meant.

On the other hand, she may merely have meant, "Everything is copy."

When she was in the hospital, dying, she said to me, "You're a reporter, Nora. Take notes." It seems to me this is not quite the same as "Everything is copy."

My mother died of cirrhosis, but the immediate cause of her death was an overdose of sleeping pills administered by my father. At the time this didn't seem to me to fall under the rubric of "Everything is copy." Although it did to my sister Amy, and she put it into a novel. Who can blame her?

How she died: my version

My mother is in the hospital. Every day, my father calls and says, this is it, they're pulling the plug. But there is no plug. My mother comes home. Several days pass. One day my father says, I'm going to give the nurse the night off. Late that night, he calls to tell me my mother has died. The funeral home has already come and taken away her body. I go to their apartment. It's four in the morning. I sit with my father for a while, and then we both decide to take a nap before the next day begins. My father reaches into the pocket of his bathrobe and pulls out a bottle of sleeping pills. "The doctor gave me these in case I was having trouble sleeping," he says. "Flush them down the toilet." I go into the bathroom and flush them down the toilet. The next morning, when my sisters arrive, I tell them about the pills. My sister Amy says to me, "Did you count the pills?"

"No," I say.

"Duh," she says.

I was married to him for six years

My first husband is a perfectly nice person, although he's pathologically attached to his cats. It's 1972, the height of the women's movement, and everyone is getting a divorce, even people whose husbands don't have pathological attachments to their cats. My husband is planning for us to take a photo safari through Africa, and I say to him, "I can't go on this trip."

"Why not?" he says.

"Because it's very expensive and we're probably going to split up and I'll feel horribly guilty that you spent all this money taking me to Africa."

"Don't be crazy," my husband says. "I love you and you love me and we're not getting a divorce and even if we do, you're the only person I want to go to Africa with. We're going."

So we go to Africa. It's a wonderful trip. When we come back, I tell my husband that I want a divorce. "But I took you to Africa!" he says.

You can't make this stuff up

I'm working on a magazine story about a woman who was fired from her job as president of Bennington

College. I have read a story about her in *The New York Times* that says she's been fired—along with her husband, the vice president of Bennington—because of her brave stand against tenure. I suspect her firing has nothing to do with her brave stand against tenure, although I don't have a clue what the real reason is. I go to Bennington and discover that she has in fact been fired because she's been having an affair with a professor at Bennington, that they taught a class in Hawthorne together, and that they both wore matching T-shirts in class with scarlet *A*'s on them. What's more, I learn that the faculty hated her from the very beginning because she had a party for them and served lukewarm lasagna and unthawed Sara Lee banana cake. I can't get over this aspect of journalism. I can't believe how real life never lets you down. I can't understand why anyone would write fiction when what actually happens is so amazing.

Everything is copy

I'm seven months pregnant with my second child, and I've just discovered that my second husband is in love with someone else. She too is married. Her husband telephones me. He's the British ambassador to the United States. I'm not kidding. He happens to be the kind of person who tends to see almost everything in global terms. He suggests lunch. We meet outside a Chinese restaurant on Connecticut Avenue and fall into each other's arms, weeping. "Oh, Peter," I say to him, "isn't it awful?"

"It's awful," he says. "What's happening to this country?"

I'm crying hysterically, but I'm thinking, someday this will be a funny story.

I was married to him for two years and eight months

I fly to New York to see my shrink. I walk into her office and burst into tears. I tell her what my husband has done to me. I tell her my heart is broken. I tell her I'm a total mess and I will never be the same. I can't stop crying. She looks at me and says, "You have to understand something: You were going to leave him eventually."

On the other hand, perhaps you can make this stuff up

So I write a novel. I change my first husband's cats into hamsters, and I change the British ambassador into an undersecretary of state, and I give my second husband a beard.

One of the saddest things about divorce

My sister Delia says this, and it's true. When we were growing up, we used to love to hear the story of how our parents met and fell in love and eloped one summer when they were both camp counselors. It was so much a part of our lives, a song sung again and again, and no matter what happened, no matter how awful things became between the two of them, we always knew that our parents had once been madly in love.

But in a divorce, you never tell your children that you were once madly in love with their father because it would be too confusing.

And then, after a while, you can't even remember whether you were.

A man and a woman live in a house
on a deserted peninsula

Alice Arlen and I have written a script for the movie *Silkwood*. It's based on the true story of Karen Silkwood, who worked at a plutonium plant in Oklahoma; she died in a mysterious automobile accident while on her way to meet a *New York Times* reporter to talk about conditions in the plant. Mike Nichols is going to direct it; he was supposed to direct a Broadway musical instead, but it all fell through because he was betrayed by a close friend who was involved with the show. We will call the close friend Jane Doe for the purposes of this story.

So we all start to work together on the next draft of the script, and Mike keeps suggesting scenes for the movie that involve Karen Silkwood's being betrayed by a close woman friend. He has a million ideas along these lines, none of which really bear any resemblance to what happened to Karen Silkwood but all of which bear a resemblance to what happened between Mike and his friend Jane. I finally say, "Mike, Jane Doe did not kill Karen Silkwood."

"Yes," Mike says, "I see what you're saying. It's the peninsula story."

And he tells us the peninsula story:

A man and a woman live in a house on a deserted peninsula. The man's mother comes to stay with them, and the man goes off on a business trip. The woman takes the ferry to the mainland and goes to see her lover. They make love. When they finish, she realizes it's late, and she gets up, dresses, and rushes to catch the last ferry home. But she misses the boat. She pleads with the ferryboat captain. He tells her he will take her back to the peninsula if she gives him six times the normal fare. But she doesn't have the money. So she's forced to walk home, and on the way, she's raped and killed by a stranger.

And the question is: Who is responsible for her death, and in what order—the woman, the man, the mother, the ferryboat captain, the lover, or the rapist?

The question is a Rorschach, Mike says, and if you ask your friends to answer it, they will all answer differently.

Another lightbulb moment.

This one marks the end of my love affair with journalism and the beginning of my understanding that just about everything is a story.

The Story of My Life in 3,500 Words or Less

Or, as E. L. Doctorow once wrote, far more succinctly

"I am led to the proposition that there is no fiction or nonfiction as we commonly understand the distinction; there is only narrative."

From my script for <u>When Harry Met Sally</u>

HARRY
Why don't you tell me the story of your life?

SALLY
The story of my life?

HARRY
We've got eighteen hours to kill before we hit New York.

SALLY
The story of my life isn't even going to get us out of Chicago. I mean, nothing's happened to me yet. That's why I'm going to New York.

HARRY
So something can happen to you?

SALLY
Yes.

HARRY
Like what?

SALLY

Like I'm going to go to journalism school to become a reporter.

HARRY

So you can write about things that happen to other people.

SALLY

That's one way to look at it.

HARRY

Suppose nothing happens to you? Suppose you live there your whole life and nothing happens. You never meet anyone, you never become anything, and finally you die one of those New York deaths where nobody notices for two weeks until the smell drifts out into the hallway?

A guy walks into a restaurant

I'm having dinner at a restaurant with friends. A man I know comes over to the table. He's a famously nice guy. His marriage broke up at about the same time mine did. He says, "How can I find you?"

.   .   .

We can't do everything

I'm sitting in a small screening room waiting for a movie to begin. The room fills up. There aren't enough seats. People are bunching up in the aisles and looking around helplessly. I'm next to my friend Bob Gottlieb, watching all this. The director of the movie decides to solve the problem by asking all the children at the screening to share seats. I watch in mounting frustration. Finally, I say to Bob, "It's really very simple. Someone should go get some folding chairs and set them up in the aisles."

Bob looks at me. "Nora," he says, "we can't do everything."

My brain clears in an amazing way.

Nora. We can't do everything.

I have been given the secret of life.

Although it's probably a little late.

And by the way

The other day I bought a red coat, on sale. But I haven't worn it yet.

The Lost Strudel or
Le Strudel Perdu

Food vanishes.

I don't mean food as habit, food as memory, food as biography, food as metaphor, food as regret, food as love, or food as in those famous madeleines people like me are constantly referring to as if they've read Proust, which in most cases they haven't. I mean food as food. Food vanishes.

I'm talking about cabbage strudel, which vanished from Manhattan in about 1982 and which I've been searching for these last twenty-three years.

The Lost Strudel *or* Le Strudel Perdu

Cabbage strudel is on a long list of things I loved to eat that used to be here and then weren't, starting with frozen custard; this delectable treat vanished when I was five years old, when my family moved to California, and my life has been a series of little heartbreaks ever since.

The cabbage strudel I'm writing about was sold at an extremely modest Hungarian bakery on Third Avenue called Mrs. Herbst's. I initially tasted it in 1968, and I don't want to be sentimental about it except to say that it's almost the only thing I remember about my first marriage. Cabbage strudel looks like apple strudel but it's not a dessert; it's more like a *pirozhok,* the meat-stuffed puff pastry that was a specialty of the Russian Tea Room, which also vanished. It's served with soup, or with a main course like pot roast or roast pheasant (not that I've ever made roast pheasant, but no question cabbage strudel would be delicious with it). It has a buttery, flaky, crispy strudel crust made of phyllo (the art of which I plan to master in my next life, when I will also read Proust past the first chapter), with a moist filling of sautéed cabbage that's simultaneously sweet, savory, and completely unexpected, like all good things. Once upon a time I ate quite a lot of cabbage strudel, and then I sort of forgot about it for a while. I think of that period as my own personal *temps perdu,* and I feel bad about it for many reasons, not the least of which is that it never crossed my mind that my beloved cabbage strudel would not be waiting for me when I was ready to remember it again.

This is New York, of course. The city throws curves. Rents go up. People get old and their children no longer want to run the store. So you find yourself on the East Side looking for Mrs. Herbst's Hungarian bakery, which was there, has always been there, is a landmark for God's sake, a fixture of the neighborhood, practically a defining moment of New York life, and it's vanished and no one even bothered to tell you. It's sad. Not as sad as things that are truly sad, I'll grant you that, but sad nonetheless. On the other hand, the full blow is mitigated somewhat by the possibility that somewhere, somehow, you'll find the lost strudel, or be able to replicate it. And so, at first, you hope. And then, you hope against hope. And then finally, you lose hope. And there you have it: the three stages of grief when it comes to lost food.

The strudel was not to be found. I spent hours on the Internet looking for a recipe, but nothing seemed like the exact cabbage strudel I'd lost. At a cocktail party, I lunged pathetically at a man named Peter Herbst, a magazine editor who my husband had led me to believe was a relative of the Herbst strudel dynasty, but he turned out not to be. I spoke to George Lang, the famous Hungarian restaurateur, who was kind enough to send me a recipe for cabbage strudel, but I tried making it and it just wasn't the same. (The truth is, most of the genuinely tragic episodes of lost food are things that are somewhat outside the reach of the home cook, even a home cook like me who has been known to overreach from time to time.)

The Lost Strudel *or* Le Strudel Perdu

About two years ago, when I had landed in what I thought was the slough of despond where cabbage strudel was concerned and could not possibly sink lower, my heart was broken once again: the food writer Ed Levine told me that the strudel I was looking for was available, by special order only, at a Hungarian bakery named Andre's in Rego Park, Queens. Ed hadn't actually sampled it himself, but he assured me that all I had to do was call Andre and he'd make it for me. I couldn't believe it. I immediately called Andre. I dropped Ed Levine's name so hard you could hear it in New Jersey. I said that Ed had told me Andre would make cabbage strudel if I ordered it, so I was calling to order it. I was prepared to order a gross of cabbage strudels if necessary. Guess what? Andre didn't care about Ed Levine or me. He refused to make it. He said he was way too busy making other kinds of strudel. So that was that.

But it wasn't.

This week, I heard from Ed Levine again. He e-mailed to say that Andre's Hungarian bakery had opened a branch in Manhattan, on Second Avenue and Eighty-fifth Street. It was selling cabbage strudel over the counter. You didn't even have to order it, it was sitting right there in the bakery case. Ed Levine had eaten a piece of it. "Now I understand why you've been raving about cabbage strudel all this time," he wrote.

The next day my husband and I walked over to Andre's. It was a beautiful winter day in New York—or my idea of a beautiful winter day, in that you barely needed a coat. We found the bakery, which is also a café, went inside and ordered the cabbage strudel, heated up. It arrived. I lifted a forkful to my lips and tasted it.

Now I'm not going to tell you that (like Proust tasting the madeleine) I shuddered; nor am I going to report that "the vicissitudes of life had become indifferent to me, its disasters innocuous, its brevity illusory." That would take way more than cabbage strudel. But Andre's cabbage strudel was divine—crisp but moist, savory but sweet, buttery beyond imagining. It wasn't completely identical to Mrs. Herbst's, but it was absolutely as delicious, if not more so. Tasting it again was like being able to turn back the clock, like having the consequences of a mistake erased; it was better than getting a blouse back that the dry cleaners had lost, or a cell phone returned that had been left in a taxi; it was a validation of never-giving-up and of hope-springing-eternal; it was many things, it was all things, it was nothing at all; but mostly, it was cabbage strudel.

On Rapture

I've just surfaced from spending several days in a state of rapture—with a book. I loved this book. I loved every second of it. I was transported into its world. I was reminded of all sorts of things in my own life. I was in anguish over the fate of its characters. I felt alive, and engaged, and positively brilliant, bursting with ideas, brimming with memories of other books I've loved. I composed a dozen imaginary letters to the author, letters I'll never write, much less send. I wrote letters of praise. I wrote letters relating entirely inappropriate personal information about my own experiences with the author's subject matter. I even wrote a letter of recrimination when one of the characters died and I was grief-stricken. But mostly I wrote letters of gratitude: the state of rapture I experience when I read a wonderful book is one of the main reasons I read, but it doesn't happen every time or even every other time, and when it does happen, I'm truly beside myself.

When I was a child, nearly every book I read sent me into rapture. Can I be romanticizing my early reading experiences? I don't think so. I can tick off so many books that I read and re-read when I was growing up— foremost among them the Oz books, which obsessed me—but so many others that were favorites in the most compelling way. I wanted so badly to *be* Jane Banks, growing up in London with Mary Poppins for a nanny, or Homer Price, growing up in Centerburg with an uncle who owned a donut machine that wouldn't stop making donuts. Little Sara Crewe in Frances Hodgson Burnett's classic *A Little Princess* was my alter ego—not in any real way, you understand; she was a much better-behaved child than I ever was—but I was so entranced by the story of the little rich girl who was sent up to the garret to be the scullery maid at the fancy boarding school where she'd been a pampered student before her father died. Oh, how I wanted to be an orphan! I read *The Nun's Story,* and oh, how I wanted to be a nun! I wanted to be shipwrecked on a desert island and stranded in Krakatoa! I wanted to be Ozma, and Jo March, and Anne Frank, and Nancy Drew, and Eloise, and Anne of Green Gables—and in my imagination, at least, I could be.

I did most of my reading as a child on my bed or on a rattan sofa in the sunroom of the house I grew up in. Here's a strange thing: Whenever I read a book I love, I start to remember all the other books that have sent me into rapture, and I can remember where I was living and the couch I was sitting on when I read them. After college, living in Greenwich Village, I sat on my brand-new wide-wale corduroy couch and read *The Golden Notebook* by Doris Lessing, the extraordinary novel that changed my life and the lives of so many other young women in the 1960s. I have the paperback copy I read at the time, and it's dog-eared, epiphany after epiphany marked so that I could easily refer back to them. Does anyone read *The Golden Notebook* nowadays? I don't know, but at the time, just before the second stage of the women's movement burst into being, I was electrified by Lessing's heroine, Anna, and her struggle to become a free woman. Work, friendship, love, sex, politics, psychoanalysis, writing—all the things that preoccupied me were Lessing's subjects, and I can remember how many times I put the book down, reeling from its brilliance and insights.

Cut to a few years later. The couch is covered with purple slipcovers, and I'm reading for pure pleasure—it's *The Godfather* by Mario Puzo, a divine book that sweeps me off into a wave of romantic delirium. I want to be a mafioso! No, that's not quite right. Okay then, I want to be a mafioso's wife!

A few years later, I'm divorced. No surprise there. The couch and I have moved to a dark apartment in the West Fifties. It's a summer weekend, I have nothing

whatsoever to do, and I should be lonely but I'm not—
I'm reading the collected works of Raymond Chandler.

Six years later, another divorce. For weeks I've been
unable to focus, to settle down, to read anything at all. A
friend I'm staying with gives me the bound galleys of
Smiley's People. I sink into bed in the guest bedroom and
happily surrender to John le Carré. I love John le Carré,
but I'm even more in love with his hero, George Smiley,
the spy with the broken heart. I want George Smiley to
get over his broken heart. I want him to get over his horrible ex-wife who betrayed him. I want George Smiley to
fall in love. I want George Smiley to fall in love with me.
George Smiley, come to think of it, is exactly the sort of
person I ought to marry and never do. I make a mental
note to write John le Carré a letter giving him the bene-
fit of my wisdom on this score.

But meanwhile, my purple couch is lost in the
divorce and I buy a new couch, a wonderful squishy
thing covered with a warm, cozy fabric, with arms you
can lie back on and cushions you can sink into, depending on whether you want to read sitting up or lying
down. On it I read most of Anthony Trollope and all of
Edith Wharton, both of whom are dead and can't be written to. Too bad; I'd like to tell them their books are as
contemporary as they were when they were written. I
read all of Jane Austen, six novels back to back, and
spend days blissfully worrying over whether the lovers
in each book will ever overcome the misunderstandings,
objections, misapprehensions, character flaws, class dis-
tinctions, and all the other obstacles to love. I read these

novels in a state of suspense so intense that you would never guess I have read them all at least ten times before.

And finally, one day, I read the novel that is probably the most rapture-inducing book of my adult life. On a chaise longue at the beach on a beautiful summer day, I open Wilkie Collins's masterpiece, *The Woman in White,* probably the first great work of mystery fiction ever written (although that description hardly does it justice), and I am instantly lost to the world. Days pass as I savor every word. Each minute I spend away from the book pretending to be interested in everyday life is a misery. How could I have waited so long to read this book? When can I get back to it? Halfway through, I return to New York to work, to finish a movie, and I sit in the mix studio unable to focus on anything but whether my favorite character in the book will survive. I will not be able to bear it if anything bad happens to my beloved Marian Halcombe. Every so often I look up from the book and see a roomful of people waiting for me to make a decision about whether the music is too soft or the thunder is too loud, and I can't believe they don't understand that what I'm doing is Much More Important. I'm reading the most wonderful book.

There's something called the rapture of the deep, and it refers to what happens when a deep-sea diver spends too much time at the bottom of the ocean and can't tell which way is up. When he surfaces, he's liable to have a condition called the bends, where the body can't adapt to the oxygen levels in the atmosphere. All

this happens to me when I surface from a great book.
The book I've currently surfaced from—the one I men-
tioned at the beginning of this piece—is called *The
Amazing Adventures of Kavalier and Clay* by Michael
Chabon. It's about two men who create comic-book characters, but it's also about how artists create fantastic
and magical things from the events of everyday life. At
one point in the book there's a roomful of moths, and
then a few pages later there's a huge luna moth sitting
in a maple tree in Union Square Park—and all of this is
reinvented a few pages later as a female comic-book
heroine named Luna Moth. The moment where the
image turns from ordinary to fantastic was so magical
that I had to put down the book. I was dazed by the play-
fulness of the author and his ability to do something so
difficult with such apparent ease. Chabon's novel takes
place in New York City in the 1940s, and though I finished reading it more than a week ago, I'm still there.
I'm smoking Camels, and Salvador Dalí is at a party in
the next room. Eventually, I'll have to start breathing
the air in today's New York again, but on the other hand,
perhaps I won't have to. I'll find another book I love and
disappear into it. Wish me luck.

What I Wish I'd Known

People have only one way to be.

Buy, don't rent.

Never marry a man you wouldn't want to be divorced from.

Don't cover a couch with anything that isn't more or less beige.

Don't buy anything that is 100 percent wool even if it seems to be very soft and not particularly itchy when you try it on in the store.

You can't be friends with people who call after 11 p.m.

Block everyone on your instant mail.

The world's greatest babysitter burns out after two and a half years.

You never know.

The last four years of psychoanalysis are a waste of money.

The plane is not going to crash.

Anything you think is wrong with your body at the age of thirty-five you will be nostalgic for at the age of forty-five.

At the age of fifty-five you will get a saggy roll just above your waist even if you are painfully thin.

This saggy roll just above your waist will be especially visible from the back and will force you to reevaluate half the clothes in your closet, especially the white shirts.

Write everything down.

What I Wish I'd Known

Keep a journal.

Take more pictures.

The empty nest is underrated.

You can order more than one dessert.

You can't own too many black turtleneck sweaters.

If the shoe doesn't fit in the shoe store, it's never going to fit.

When your children are teenagers, it's important to have a dog so that someone in the house is happy to see you.

Back up your files.

Overinsure everything.

Whenever someone says the words "Our friendship is more important than this," watch out, because it almost never is.

There's no point in making piecrust from scratch.

The reason you're waking up in the middle of the night is the second glass of wine.

The minute you decide to get divorced, go see a lawyer and file the papers.

125

Overtip.

Never let them know.

If only one third of your clothes are mistakes, you're ahead of the game.

If friends ask you to be their child's guardian in case they die in a plane crash, you can say no.

There are no secrets.

Considering the Alternative

When I turned sixty, I had a big birthday party in Las Vegas, which happens to be one of my top five places. We spent the weekend eating and drinking and gambling and having fun. One of my friends threw twelve passes at the craps table and we all made some money and screamed and yelled and I went to bed deliriously happy. The spell lasted for several days, and as a result, I managed to avoid thinking about what it all meant. Denial has been a way of life for me for many years. I actually believe in denial. It seemed to me that the only way to deal with a birthday of this sort was to do everything possible to push it from my mind. Nothing else about me is better than it was at fifty, or forty, or thirty, but I definitely have the best haircut I've ever had, I like my new apartment, and, as the expression goes, consider the alternative.

I have been sixty for four years now, and by the time you read this I will probably have been sixty for five. I survived turning sixty, I was not thrilled to turn sixty-one, I was less thrilled to turn sixty-two, I didn't much like being sixty-three, I loathed being sixty-four, and I will hate being sixty-five. I don't let on about such things in person; in person, I am cheerful and Pollyannaish. But the honest truth is that it's sad to be over sixty. The long shadows are everywhere—friends dying and battling illness. A miasma of melancholy hangs there, forcing you to deal with the fact that your life, however happy and successful, has been full of disappointments and mistakes, little ones and big ones. There are dreams that are never quite going to come true, ambitions that will never quite be realized. There are, in short, regrets. Edith Piaf was famous for singing a song called "Non, je ne regrette rien." It's a good song. I know what she meant. I can get into it; I can make a case that I regret nothing. After all, most of my mistakes turned out to be things I survived, or turned into funny stories, or, on occasion, even made money from. But the truth is that *je regrette beaucoup.*

There are all sorts of books written for older women. They are, as far as I can tell, uniformly upbeat and full of

bromides and homilies about how pleasant life can be
once one is free from all the nagging obligations of children, monthly periods, and, in some cases, full-time jobs.
I find these books utterly useless, just as I found all the
books I once read about menopause utterly useless. Why
do people write books that say it's better to be older than
to be younger? It's not better. Even if you have all your
marbles, you're constantly reaching for the name of the
person you met the day before yesterday. Even if you're
in great shape, you can't chop an onion the way you used
to and you can't ride a bicycle several miles without
becoming a candidate for traction. If you work, you're
surrounded by young people who are plugged into the
marketplace, the demographic, the zeitgeist; they want
your job and someday soon they're going to get it. If
you're fortunate enough to be in a sexual relationship, you're not going to have the sex you once had. Plus,
you can't wear a bikini. Oh, how I regret not having
worn a bikini for the entire year I was twenty-six. If anyone young is reading this, go, right this minute, put on a
bikini, and don't take it off until you're thirty-four.

A magazine editor called me the other day, an editor
who, like me, is over sixty. Her magazine was going to do
an issue on Age, and she wanted me to write something
for it. We began to talk about the subject, and she said,
"You know what drives me nuts? Why do women our age
say, 'In my day . . .'? *This* is our day."

But it isn't our day. It's *their* day. We're just hanging
on. We can't wear tank tops, we have no idea who 50 Cent
is, and we don't know how to use almost any of the func-

tions on our cell phones. If we hit the wrong button on the remote control and the television screen turns to snow, we have no idea how to get the television set back to where it was in the first place. (This is the true nightmare of the empty nest: Your children are gone, and they were the only people in the house who knew how to use the remote control.) Technology is a bitch. I can no longer even figure out how to get the buttons on the car radio to play my favorite stations. The gears on my bicycle mystify me. On my bicycle! And thank God no one has given me a digital wristwatch. In fact, if any of my friends are reading this, please don't ever give me a digital anything.

Just the other day I went shopping at a store in Los Angeles that happens to stock jeans that actually come all the way up to my waist, and I was stunned to discover that the customer just before me was Nancy Reagan. That's how old I am: Nancy Reagan and I shop in the same store.

Anyway, I said to this editor, you're wrong, you are so wrong, this is not *our* day, this is *their* day. But she was undaunted. She said to me, well then, I have another idea: Why don't you write about Age Shame? I said to her, get someone who is only fifty to write about Age Shame. I am way past Age Shame, if I ever had it. I'm just happy to be here at all.

Anyway, the point is, I don't know why so much nonsense about age is written—although I can certainly understand that no one really wants to read anything that says aging sucks. We are a generation that has learned to believe we can do something about almost everything. We are active—hell, we are proactive. We are positive thinkers. We have the power. We will take any suggestion seriously. If a pill will help, we will take it. If being in the Zone will help, we will enter the Zone. When we hear about the latest ludicrously expensive face cream that is alleged to turn back the clock, we will go out and buy it even though we know that the last five face creams we fell for were completely ineffectual. We will do crossword puzzles to ward off Alzheimer's and eat six almonds a day to ward off cancer; we will scan ourselves to find whatever can be nipped in the bud. We are in control. Behind the wheel. On the cutting edge. We make lists. We seek out the options. We surf the net.

But there are some things that are absolutely, definitively, entirely uncontrollable.

I am dancing around the D word, but I don't mean to be coy. When you cross into your sixties, your odds of dying—or of merely getting horribly sick on the way to dying—spike. Death is a sniper. It strikes people you love, people you like, people you know, it's everywhere. You could be next. But then you turn out not to be. But then again you could be.

Meanwhile, your friends die, and you're left not just bereft, not just grieving, not just guilty, but utterly helpless. There is nothing you can do. Everybody dies.

"What is the answer?" Gertrude Stein asked Alice B. Toklas as Stein was dying.

There was no reply.

"In that case, what is the question?" Stein asked.

Well, exactly.

Well, not quite exactly. Here are some questions I am constantly noodling over: Do you splurge or do you hoard? Do you live every day as if it's your last, or do you save your money on the chance you'll live twenty more years? Is life too short, or is it going to be too long? Do you work as hard as you can, or do you slow down to smell the roses? And where do carbohydrates fit into all this? Are we really going to have to spend our last years avoiding bread, especially now that bread in America is so unbelievably delicious? And what about chocolate? There's a question for you, Gertrude Stein—what about chocolate?

My friend Judy died last year. She was the person I told everything to. She was my best friend, my extra sister, my true mother, sometimes even my daughter, she was all these things, and one day she called up to say, the weirdest thing has happened, there's a lump on my tongue. Less than a year later, she was dead. She was sixty-six years old. She had no interest in dying, right to the end. She died horribly. And now she's gone. I think of her every day, sometimes six or seven times a day. This is the weekend she and I usually went to the spring garden and antiques show in Bridgehampton together. The fire screen in the next room is something she spotted in a corner of that antiques show, and above the fireplace is a poster of a seagull that she gave me only two summers ago. It's June now; this is the month one or the other of us would make corn-bread pudding, a ridiculous recipe we both loved that's made with corn-bread mix and canned cream corn. She made hers with sour cream, and I made mine without. "Hi, hon," she would say when she called. "Hi, doll." "Hello, my darling." I don't think she ever called me, or anyone else she knew, by their actual name. I have her white cashmere shawl. I wore it for days after her death; I wrapped myself up in it; I even slept in it. But now I can't bear to wear it because it feels as if that's all there is left of my Judy. I want to talk to her. I want to have lunch with her. I want her to give me a book she just read and loved. She is my phantom limb, and I can't believe I'm here without her.

A few months before they found the lump on her tongue, Judy and I went out to lunch to celebrate a friend's birthday. It had been a difficult year: barely a week had passed without some terrible news about someone's health. I said at lunch, What are we going to do about this? Shouldn't we talk about this? This is what our lives have become. Death is everywhere. How do we deal with it? Our birthday friend said, oh, please, let's not be morbid.

Yes. Let's not be morbid.

Let's not.

On the other hand, I meant to have a conversation with Judy about death. Before either of us was sick or dying. I meant to have one of those straightforward conversations where you discuss What You Want in the eventuality—well, I say "the eventuality," but that's one of the oddest things about this whole subject. Death doesn't really feel eventual or inevitable. It still feels . . . avoidable somehow. But it's not. We know in one part of our brains that we are all going to die, but on some level we don't quite believe it.

But I meant to have that conversation with Judy, so that when the inevitable happened we would know what our intentions were, so that we could help each other die in whatever way we wanted to die. But of course, once they found the lump, there was no having the conversation. Living wills are much easier to draft when you are living instead of possibly dying; they're the ultimate hypotheticals. And what difference would it have made if we'd had that conversation? Before you get sick, you have absolutely no idea of how you're going to feel once you do. You can imagine you'll be brave, but it's just as possible you'll be terrified. You can hope that you'll find a way to accept death, but you could just as easily end up raging against it. You have no idea what your particular prognosis is going to be, or how you'll react to it, or what options you'll have. You have no clue whether you will ever even know the truth about your prognosis, because the real question is, What is the truth, and who is going to tell it to us, and are we even going to want to hear it?

My friend Henry died a few months ago. He was what we refer to as one of the lucky ones. He died at eighty-two, having lived a full, rich, and successful life. He had coped brilliantly with macular degeneration— for almost two years, most of his friends had no idea he couldn't see—and then he wrote a book about going blind that will probably outlast all the rest of his accomplishments, which were considerable. He died of heart failure, peacefully, in his sleep, with his adoring family around him. The day before his death, he asked to be brought a large brown accordion folder he kept in his office. In it were love letters he had received when he was younger. He sent them back to the women who'd written them, wrote them all lovely notes, and destroyed the rest. What's more, he left complete, detailed instructions for his funeral, including the music he wanted—all of this laid out explicitly in a file on his computer he called "Exit."

I so admire Henry and the way he handled his death. It's inspirational. And yet I can't quite figure out how any of it applies. For one thing, I have managed to lose all my love letters. Not that there were that many. And if I ever found them and sent them back to the men who wrote them to me, I promise you they would be completely mystified. I haven't heard from any of these men in years, and on the evidence, they all seem to have done an extremely good job of getting over me. As for instructions for my funeral, I suppose I could come up with a few. For example, if there's a reception afterward, I know what sort of food I would like served: those little finger sandwiches from this place on Lexington Avenue called William Poll. And champagne would be nice. I love champagne. It's so festive. But otherwise I don't have a clue. I haven't even figured out whether I want to be buried or cremated—largely because I've always worried that cremation in some way lowers your chances of being reincarnated. (If there is such a thing.) (Which I know there isn't.) (And yet.)

"I don't want to die," Judy said.

"I believe in miracles," she said.

"I love you," she said.

"Can you believe this?" she said.

No, I can't believe it. I still can't believe it.

But let's not be morbid.

Let's put little smiley faces on our faces.

LOL.

Eat, drink, and be merry.

Seize the day.

Life goes on.

It could be worse.

And the ever popular "Consider the alternative."

And meanwhile, here we are.

What is to be done?

I don't know. I hope that's clear. In a few minutes I will be through with writing this piece, and I will go back to life itself. Squirrels have made a hole in the roof, and we don't quite know what to do about it. Soon it will rain; we should probably take the cushions inside. I need more bath oil. And that reminds me to say something about bath oil. I use this bath oil I happen to love. It's called Dr. Hauschka's lemon bath. It costs about twenty dollars a bottle, which is enough for about two weeks of baths if you follow the instructions. The instructions say one capful per bath. But a capful gets you nowhere. A capful is not enough. I have known this for a long time. But if the events of the last few years have taught me anything, it's that I'm going to feel like an idiot if I die tomorrow and I skimped on bath oil today. So I use quite a lot of bath oil. More than you could ever imagine. After I take a bath, my bathtub is as dangerous as an oil slick. But thanks to the bath oil, I'm as smooth as silk. I am going out to buy more, right now. Goodbye.

Acknowledgments

Thanks to Amanda Urban, Delia Ephron, Jerome Kass, David Remnick, Amy Gross, Shelley Wanger, and Bob Gottlieb.

I would also like to thank all the people who have labored hard to stop the forces of gravity where I'm concerned. As a result I look approximately one year younger than I am. You know who you are.

A NOTE ABOUT THE AUTHOR

Nora Ephron is the author of *Crazy Salad, Heartburn, Wallflower at the Orgy,* and *Scribble Scribble.* She has received Academy Award nominations for Best Original Screenplay for *When Harry Met Sally, Silkwood,* and *Sleepless in Seattle,* which she also directed. Her other credits include the films *Michael* and *Bewitched* and the play *Imaginary Friends.* She lives in New York City with her husband, writer Nicholas Pileggi.

A NOTE ON THE TYPE

The text of this book was set in Century Schoolbook, one of several variations of Century Roman to appear within a decade of its creation. The original Century Roman face was cut by Linn Boyd Benton (1844–1932) in 1895, in response to a request by Theodore Low De Vinne for an attractive, easy-to-read typeface to fit the narrow columns of his *Century Magazine*.

Century Schoolbook was specifically designed for school textbooks in the primary grades, but its great legibility quickly earned it popularity in a range of applications. Century remains the only American face cut before 1910 that is still widely in use today.

Composed by Creative Graphics,
Allentown, Pennsylvania

Printed and bound by R. R. Donnelley and Sons,
Harrisonburg, Virginia

Designed by Soonyoung Kwon

3-16